D0516101

NATIONS of the WORLD

SAMUEL BRIMSON

Library of Congress Cataloging-in-Publication Data available
upon request from publisher. Fax (414) 336-0157 for the attention
of the Publishing Records Department.

ISBN 0-8368-5488-8

This North American edition first published in 2004 by
World Almanac® Library,
330 West Olive Street, Suite 100, Milwaukee, WI 53212 USA.

Created by Trocadero Publishing, an Electra Media Group
Enterprise, Suite 204, 74 Pitt Street, Sydney NSW 2000, Australia.

Original copyright © 2003 S. and L. Brodie.

WORLD ALMANAC® LIBRARY

Hungary

REPUBLIC OF HUNGARY

Hungary is a landlocked nation in central Europe. The Alföld, or Great Hungarian Plain, makes up about half of the landscape. Through it flows the Danube River, the main waterway of Hungary. Relatively low mountains run from the southwest to the northeast, where they meet the Carpathian Mountains. The climate is continental with warm summers and cold winters.

More than ninety percent of the population is made up of Magyar people, but this has been the case only since World War II. Previously there was a greater mix of ethnic backgrounds, including Slav and Romanian. Today, there are Gypsy, German, Slovak and Romanian minorities.

Most Hungarians are Christian. There is a small Jewish population and a tiny number of Muslims. Magyar is the principal language, though much of the Gypsy population speaks Romanian.

The economy of Hungary was almost solely dependent upon agriculture prior to World-War II. The Communists took power in 1948. They began large-scale development of the country's heavy industries. The production of consumer goods for export was extremely limited. Massive reforms, beginning in the late 1980s, saw a widespread conversion to free market principles. The emphasis changed from producing goods for the Soviet Union to serving the international market. The principal manufacturing industries are steel, chemicals, cement, processed foods, motor vehicles and pharmaceuticals. About thirty percent of the people now work in manufacturing. Hungary today has one of eastern Europe's most successful economies.

The key agricultural crops are wheat, barley, corn, sunflower seeds, grapes, beet sugar and potatoes. The wines made from Hungarian grapes have brought international acclaim. Sheep, cattle and pigs are the main farming livestock.

The nation's substantial mineral resources include copper, coal, oil, natural gas, uranium and bauxite. Forestry, once a major part of the Hungarian economy, is limited due to poor reforestation in the past.

The Danube River flows through the heart of Budapest, Hungary's capital.

A village store with dried peppers on sale.

SCOTT BRODIE

Hungary's constitution was adopted in 1949. It was amended in 1972, 1989 and 1997. Hungary has a unicameral National Assembly whose members are elected by the people for four-year terms. The president is head of state while the prime minister is head of government. The National Assembly elects the president for a maximum of two five-year terms. The prime minister is chosen by the National Assembly upon the recommendation of the president.

The Roman Empire conquered the provinces of Pannonia and Dacia, the present Hungary, in the first century A.D. In the fourth century Hungary was overrun by Huns, and subsequently by Ostro-

goths and Avars. Magyars crossed the Ural Mountains to settle in Hungary in the ninth century.

The Magyars integrated with the existing population. They proceeded to expand their domain westward under the chieftain Arpad. Holy Roman Emperor Otto I defeated the Magyars in 955. Christianity was adopted as the national religion. Stephen I, named king by Pope Sylvester II in 1001, led the Arpad dynasty of Hungary until 1038.

King Stephen's successors faced a number of invasions which weakened the kingdom. King Ladislas I arranged a new alliance with Rome to strengthen the kingdom. Hungary went on to conquer Slovakia, Transylvania and northern Yugoslavia.

A group of minor aristocrats forced King Andrew II to agree to the 'Golden Bull' in 1222. This was a charter which controlled the king's authority and laid the groundwork for a parliament.

A series of weak monarchs and several invasions led to the collapse of the Arpad dynasty in 1301. A group of aristocrats recruited Prince Charles Robert of Anjou as the new king. Known as Charles I, he took the throne in 1308. He restored order to the kingdom and he

GOVERNMENT
Website www.kancellaria.gov.hu
Capital Budapest
Type of government Parliamentary deocracy
Voting Universal adult suffrage
Head of state President
Head of government Prime Minister
Constitution 1949
Legislature Unicameral National Assembly (Orszaggyules)
Judiciary Constitutional Court
Member of CE, IMF, NATO, OECD, UN, UNESCO, UNHCR, WHO, WTO

LAND AND PEOPLE
Land area 35,919 sq mi (93,030 sq km)
Highest point Kekes 3,330 ft (1,015 m)
Population 10,075,034
Major cities and populations
Budapest 2,100,000
Debrecan 220,000
Miskolc 200,000
Ethnic groups Magyar 90%, Gypsie 4%, German 3%,
Religions Christianity 96%
Languages Magyar (official)

ECONOMIC
Currency Forint
Industry
mining, metallurgy, construction materials, processed foods, textiles, chemicals, pharmaceuticals, motor vehicles
Agriculture
wheat, corn, rye, sunflower seed, potatoes, beet sugar, pigs, cattle, poultry, dairy
Natural resources
bauxite, coal, natural gas

Hungary

expanded it into Bosnia and part of Serbia. His son, King Louis I, oversaw expansion of Hungarian territory into the Balkans and Poland.

Louis promoted development of commerce, science and industry. At the end of his reign, Hungary experienced many invasions by the Turks. Matthias Corvinus ruled from 1458 to 1490. He built a strong army and he made reforms to strengthen the government. He won dominion over Austria, Moravia, Silesia and Lusatia, making Hungary the strongest kingdom in Europe. Matthias limited the power of the nobles, but his successors

Classical Hungarian architecture in the streets of Budapest.

permitted them to regain a good deal of influence.

The Turks under Suleiman I conquered Hungary in 1526 in the Battle of Mohács. The next 150 years brought nearly constant strife as the Turks, the Austrian Habsburgs, and powerful nobles fought for control.

The Austrian Habsburg dynasty emerged victorious, expelling the Turks from most of Hungary with the Treaty of Karlowitz in 1699. The majority of Hungarians remained loyal to the Habsburgs for the next hundred years.

Hungarian independence movements were growing rapidly by the mid-nineteenth century. Revolutionaries declared Hungary's independence in 1849. The Habsburgs, aided by Russia, qcrushed the rebellion.

Reforms drafted in 1867 established the Austro-Hungarian monarchy, giving Hungary equality with Austria. Demands for independence grew more vehement during World War I, especially after the 1917 Russian Revolution.

Count Michael Károlyi became premier in 1918. His government soon collapsed. Communists, led by Béla Kun, took power in March 1919.

Romanian forces invaded Hungary and deposed Kun in July. They launched brutal reprisals against the communists. The Treaty of Trianon reduced Hungary's area to include only the Magyar- speaking regions.

Hungary sided with the Axis powers in World War II, hoping to regain its lost territories. The Hungarian army suffered huge losses. Believing Hungary was about to withdraw from the alliance, Germany invaded in March 1944. The Germans came under sustained attack from Soviet forces who won control by February of 1945.

A newly elected government began the process of land reform in the fall of 1945.

A typical Hungarian village.

Communists held many parliamentary seats. Premier Ferenc Nagy actually had little hope of limiting their power. Communists forced Nagy to resign after the 1947 elections. The Communists had eliminated opposition and taken control by 1954.

Conversion to a one-party communist state stirred considerable resentment among the people. An anti-communist revolt began on October 23, 1956. A new coalition government, led by Imre Nagy, declared Hungary a neutral nation. Soviet troops suppressed the movement. Hundreds of Hungarians were

The famous Chain Bridge spans the Danube River in the center of Budapest.

killed, thousands were imprisoned and nearly 200,000 fled the country.

A new Communist dictatorship was established under Premier János Kádár. The Soviet Union provided financial aid. Punishment of the former rebels continued.

Kádár ruled for more than three decades. He made numerous reforms during this time in office. Hungary increased its economic ties with non-communist nations. Increasing sums of money were needed to save Hungary's failing industries. The country faced an immense national debt. Kádár resigned in 1988.

A committee of the Parliament set forth a plan for a new

multi-party government. Kádár's former opponents worked to set up a democracy. The Soviet Union signed an agreement to reduce its involvement in 1989.

The first free multi-party elections were held in 1991. Premier József Antall began privatizing state enterprises and promoting new freedoms.

The former Communists, now calling themselves Socialists, regained power in 1994. The reform program continued as Hungary joined the North Atlantic Treaty Organization (NATO) and the European Union (EU). Socialists were elected again in 2002.

Iceland

REPUBLIC OF ICELAND

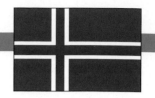

Iceland, an island in the north Atlantic Ocean, is the westernmost European country. Much of the land is plateau interspersed with over 100 volcanoes, some of which are active. Beautiful, rugged fjords line the northern coast. Fifteen percent of the landscape is snowfields and glaciers. Most people live in the lowlands of the southwest. Abundant hot springs provide heat energy. Northeastern Iceland experiences very cold and windy winters. Conditions in the southwest are more moderate.

Almost all of the population is native Icelandic and Christian. Icelandic is the national language.

Fishing and fish processing is very important to Iceland's economy. Livestock raising is a major industry. Revenue from hydroelectric power continues the grow. Iceland is one of the world's wealthiest nations.

Vikings from Norway arrived in Iceland in the ninth century, followed soon after by settlers from the British Isles. A legislature called the Althing was established in 930. The region had no head of state, but flourished for nearly three hundred years. Christianity was introduced during this time.

Civil wars raged during the thirteenth century. King Haakon of Norway used this as an opportunity to annex Iceland. Social order was restored and new laws were enacted.

Denmark conquered Norway and Iceland in 1380. The Danes set out to limit Icelandic trade with England and Germany. It forced the people to embrace Lutheranism. Iceland had lost internal political power by 1660.

Disasters reduced the population by fifty percent during the 1700s. Thousands died during a smallpox epidemic in 1707-09 and in famines soon after. Others were killed during the eruption of the Laki volcano in 1783.

Nationalism, led by scholar Jón Sigurðsson, soared in the 1800s. Denmark granted limited self-government in 1874. Great economic strides were made into the 1900s.

Icelanders voted for independence in 1944 and established a new republic on June 17th. Sveinn Björrnsson was elected president. It became a founding member of the North Atlantic Treaty Organization (NATO).

Iceland's coast guard clashed with the British navy in 1958 over the boundaries of Iceland's fishing zone. The dispute, known as the Cod Wars, was not settled until 1973.

Iceland elected the world's first woman head of state in 1980. President Vigdís Finnbogadóttir held office for sixteen years. Iceland's economic growth continues.

GOVERNMENT

Website www.iceland.org
Capital Reykjavik
Type of government Republic
Independence from Denmark
June 17,1944
Voting Universal adult suffrage
Head of state President
Head of government Prime Minister
Constitution 1944
Legislature
Unicameral Parliament (Althing)
Judiciary High Court
Member of CE, IMF, NATO, OECD, UN, UNESCO, WHO, WTO

LAND AND PEOPLE

Land area 39,769 sq mi
(103,000 sq km)
Highest point
Hvannadalshnukur
6,952 ft (2119 m)
Coastline 3,700 mi (5,955 km)
Population 279,384
Major cities and populations
Reykjavik 165,000
Kopavogur 19,000
Ethnic groups
Icelandic 98%, others 2%
Religions Christianity 95%
Languages Icelandic (official)

ECONOMIC

Currency Krona
Industry
seafood processing, aluminum smelting, ferrosilicon production, geothermal power, tourism
Agriculture
potatoes, turnips, cattle, sheep, fish
Natural resources
seafood, geothermal power, diatomite

India

REPUBLIC OF INDIA

GOVERNMENT
Website www.goidirectory.nic.in
Capital New Delhi
Type of government Republic
Independence from Britain
August 15, 1947 (dominion status)
Voting Universal adult suffrage
Head of state President
Head of government Prime Minister
Constitution 1950
Legislature
Bicameral Parliament (Sansad)
People's Assembly (Lok Sabha)
Council of States (Rajya Sabha)
Judiciary Supreme Court
Member of CN, IMF, UN, UNESCO,
UNHCR, WHO, WTO

LAND AND PEOPLE
Land area 1,269,346 sq mi
(3,287,590 sq km)
Highest point Kanchenjunga
27,858 ft (8598 m)
Coastline 4,362 mi (7,000 km)
Population 1,045,845,226
Major cities and populations
Mumbai 15.2 million
Kolkota 11.8 million
New Delhi 10 million
Ethnic groups Indo-Aryan 72%,
Dravidian 25%, others 3%
Religions
Hinduism 83%, Islam 11%, Sikh 2%,
Christianity 2%, Buddhism 1%
Languages Hindi, English (both
official), numerous others

ECONOMIC
Currency Indian rupee
Industry
tourism, motor vehicles, services,
textiles, chemicals, food processing,
steel, cement, mining, petroleum,
machinery, computer software
Agriculture
rice, wheat, oilseed, cotton, jute, tea,
sugar cane, potatoes, cattle, sheep,
goats, poultry
Natural resources
coal, iron ore, manganese, mica,
bauxite, titanium ore, chromite, natural
gas, diamonds, petroleum, limestone

Considered a subcontinent of Asia, India occupies most of the Indian Peninsula and part of the south Asian mainland. Its long coastline extends south and east from the Arabian Sea and then north to the Bay of Bengal. The northern part of India is dominated by the Himalayas, the highest mountain system in the world. These mountains are the source of the Brahmaputra, Ganges and Indus rivers.

The central region, south of the Himalayas, is an immense, fertile plain. This is the most heavily populated area due to its ample water supply and its rich soil. To the northwest of this area is the Thar Desert. Farther south is the rocky Deccan Plateau, which occupies forty percent of India's land area. The Eastern and Western Ghats mountains border opposite ends of this plateau.

India's climate varies a good deal because the country is so large. The east receives the most rainfall, the northwest the least. The climate is usually tropical, except in the mountains. The rainy season, from June to November, is the season of the southwest monsoon. Winds bring rains from the Indian Ocean and the Arabian Sea. These rains affect most of the country. The cool season, from December to February, is the season of the northeast monsoon. It brings dry weather with severe storms. The northern plains may get some rain, while the Himalayas get heavy snowfalls. The hot season runs from March to May, with temperatures as high as 125°F. (51.7° C.).

India is the second most populous country in the world. It is a land of many different ethnic groups. They are dominated by the Aryan in the north and the Dravidian in the south. The caste system classified people into different social strata in the past. While it has been outlawed, it does remain influential in daily life. Many Indian states are organized along ethnic and linguistic lines. The divisions of Indian society are more distinct in terms of language than ethnicity.

India

India is home to Hinduism. More than eighty percent of the people are Hindus. Twelve percent are Muslims. Christians and Sikhs account for two percent each.

Hindi and English are the two official national languages. Hindi, however, is spoken by only a third of the people. English speakers number even less. Indians speak more than 1600 different languages or dialects from eighteen different language groups.

India has a vast agricultural structure. Most farms are small, but there is some large-scale farming. A third of the gross domestic product comes from agriculture, which employs about sixty percent of the workforce. High rainfall provides ideal conditions for ample rice growing. Sugar cane, wheat, sorghum, jute, corn and oil seeds are the other major crops. India is also a major producer of tea. Poppies are grown legally for medicines. They are also cultivated for illicit narcotics.

India is a world leader in the production of iron ore, coal and bauxite. It also produces large amounts of mica, ilmenite, manganese, chromium, zinc, copper, gold and diamonds. Oil fields near the west coast do not produce sufficient oil to meet the nation's needs. The mountainous north is a source of oak, teak and ebony.

FLAT EARTH PICTURE GALLERY

The nation has seen major growth in manufacturing during recent decades. Much of this has come as a result of government deregulation of industries. Foreign investment has helped develop new and stronger industries.

The weaving of cotton cloth is the leading industry of India. Jute products are also major exports. The manufacture of iron and steel products has increased steadily since the 1950s. Carpet weaving, food processing, electronic, and tile production are also major industries. Handmade products include wood carvings and pottery, as well as brass, copper, and silver objects. Also important is the production of machine tools, chemicals and transportation equipment.

India's vast film industry, known as Bollywood, turns out hundreds of films each year. Service industries are growing rapidly. India is a major computer programming and software development center, providing services to major corporations around the world.

Railways and buses provide most public transport. The vast Indian railway network connects most parts of the country. There is also an extensive domestic airline network.

India is a federal republic with twenty-eight states and seven territories. Its 1949 constitution contains features of those adopted by Great Britain, the U. S. and other Western democracies. The role of president is primarily a ceremonial one. Presidents are elected for five-year terms by the members of the national and state legislatures.

The parliament is bicameral. The Council of States, or Rajya Sabha, is the upper house. Its members are elected by the state parliaments, plus twelve appointed by the president, for six-year terms. Members of the Lok Sabha, or lower house, are elected for five years by the people. The president appoints a prime minister and a cabinet, or council of ministers. Real executive power lies in the hands of the prime minister and the council of ministers.

The area now known as India was home to one of the oldest civilizations on earth. The Indus Valley civilization arose in what is now Pakistan around 2500 B.C. Its power and influence gradually spread into the area of present-day India.

While this was happening, Indo-Aryan people began migrating south from central Asia. They used the passes of the Himalayas to reach the Ganges Valley and Punjab. Eventually there was some merging of the two civilizations. The Indus Valley civilization went into decline around 1700 B.C.

Indo-Aryans became dominant, spreading over much of central India by 800 B.C. These people introduced Hinduism to the area. Of the various kingdoms that arose, the strongest was Maurya.

Alexander the Great invaded the region from 327 to 325 B.C. His forces clashed with those of Chandragupta, founder of the Maurya Empire. Eventually, they were driven out by Chandragupta.

Chandragupta's grandson, Asoka, who ruled from 272 to

The magnificent Taj Mahal at Agra.

India

232 B.C., unified most of India. Buddhism became India's principal faith under Asoka. Maurya went into decline following his death in 232 B.C. The land had split into various warring states by 185 B.C.

Indian traders began spreading east and west at this time. They established links with the Roman Empire and trading posts on the Malay peninsula and in Indonesia.

Various groups invaded the northwest in the first century B.C. The Afghans, Kushans, Parthians and Scythians all established short-lived kingdoms. The Gupta dynasty came to prominence in the north during the fourth century A.D. Peace and economic prosperity followed for many years. Learning, art and music were encouraged. Hinduism reached a new popularity as it adopted

some aspects of Buddhism. New literature was promoted. The far south was ruled by the Kallava dynasty. The Chalukyas controlled the Deccan Plateau region.

Between the eighth and thirteenth centuries many kingdoms and dynasties came to power for a time. Khorasan armies swept into the region from the northwest in 1192 A.D. They overran the region and established a Muslim sultanate at Delhi. Very quickly it exerted power over the various dynasties, except for those in the far south.

The sultanate collapsed in 1398 when Tamerlane, the Mongol conqueror, captured Delhi in 1398. The region broke up into a number of Islamic kingdoms after his withdrawal.

Babur, a descendant of Tamerlane, conquered the king-

doms one by one in the early 1500s. His victory was complete at the Battle of Panipat in 1526. He merged his conquests to form the Mughal Empire.

Emperor Akbar, the grandson of Babur, ruled from 1556 to 1605, greatly extending the empire. It reached its largest expanse under Emperor Aurangzeb, great-grandson of Akbar, who ruled until 1707. It covered all of the Indian sub-continent except for the very far south.

The first Europeans arrived in 1498 when Portuguese explorer Vasco da Gama landed at Calicut. Twelve years later Portugal annexed Goa, on the western coast, as a trading post. Its monopoly on trade with India did not last. The Dutch, French and British all sought a

Traffic congestion in Delhi.

Hawkers sell food to passengers at a railway station — trains are India's most important transport mode.

share of the Indian trade in the sixteenth century.

Britain saw the potential for huge profits in trading from India. The British East India Company was formed under a royal charter in 1600. Its first trading post was established at Surat in 1613. Other posts followed in Bombay in 1661 and Calcutta in 1691. The company was not just a trader. It had its own large naval and army forces to drive off rival traders and to control locals who resented the British.

The company was finally granted an area of land near Calcutta in 1701 by the Mughal emperor. Both Britain and France exploited the internal problems of the Mughal Empire. These included invasions from Afghanistan and internal revolts by various

Hindu sects. The European powers competed for the support of regional rulers. Britain steadily gained the upper hand.

The Nawab, or viceroy, of Bengal challenged the East India Company's growing power in his region. A military clash ensued, climaxing with the Battle of Plassey in 1757. Robert Clive led the company's army to a decisive victory to take control of Bengal's revenue. The conquest was recognized by France at the Treaty of Paris in 1763.

The Bengal example was not lost on other rulers. Most signed treaties or agreed to annexation by the company by 1818. Much of this took place under the leadership of Governor-General Warren Hastings who was appointed by the British parliament. This illus-

trates how intertwined the East India Company had become with the government of Britain. Sind and Punjab were the only states that remained independent. They eventually succumbed to Britain in 1843 and 1849 respectively.

The company usually ruled through the various princes, although they administered the larger cities directly. James Dalhousie, who became governor-general in 1848, began major road-building and irrigation schemes. His growing dominance unsettled many of the Muslim rulers.

Arrogance began to characterize much of the company's dealings. The Mughal emperor, Bahadur Shah II, was informed in 1853 that his title would cease to exist upon his death. Peasants were forced to pay taxes to fund public building projects.

Unrest had grown among the ranks of the company's army. This was particularly true of the sepoys, soldiers of Indian background. Many believed the company wanted to forcibly convert them to Christianity.

Sepoys mutinied on May 10, 1857 at Meerat, took Delhi and

India

The British governor-general became the Viceroy of India. A council of Indians was established to advise him beginning in 1861. Britain's Queen Victoria was proclaimed Empress of India in 1876. India's ultimate destiny, however, lay with the Secretary of State for India, based in London.

Indian nationalism was on the rise in the last decades of the nineteenth century. The Indian National Congress, dedicated to rule by Indians, was founded in 1885. Its dominance by Hindus prompted the formation of the Muslim League in 1906. Nationalism came to the fore when the viceroy partitioned Bengal into separate Muslim and Hindu states. The opposition was so great it was reversed after six years.

The Morley-Minto reforms of 1909 delivered increased Indian participation in the legislative process. It also established separate electorates for Muslims. This move did not please the Hindu majority.

More than 1.2 million Indians, both Hindus and Muslims, participated with Britain during World War II. The strong Indian nationalist movement resumed after the war.

Anti-British sentiment among Sikhs was inflamed in 1919 when British troops massacred hundreds of protestors at Jalianwallah Bagh. Britain passed legislation removing trial by jury in political subversion cases the same year.

At this time a young lawyer named Mohandas Gandhi rose to prominence, advocating nonviolent opposition to colonialism. Protests against the slowness of reform began in 1920, continuing into the 1930s.

Imperial conferences were held in the early 1930s. They led to the 1935 Government of India Act. Elected parliaments were established in the provinces and a federal legislature was established at Delhi. The Indian National Congress Party gained control of most of the new legislatures. Poor performance by the Muslim

proclaimed Bahadur Shah II Emperor of India. British soldiers and Sikhs, who had no love for the Mughals, crushed the mutiny in early 1858. This was the end of the Mughal Empire.

It was obvious the company was no longer equipped to govern the vast Indian region. Britain assumed direct control. It calmed the fears of the rulers of the princely states. They were guaranteed their authority and position, providing they accepted British rule. Other parts of the country came under direct colonial administration.

A Hindustan taxi waiting for a fare.

League led to demands for separate Muslim states.

The Indian Parliament withdrew from participation in government in 1939 when Britain included India in its declaration of war with Germany. The Muslim League generally cooperated with the British during the war.

Gandhi demanded Britain's withdrawal from India and launched his Quit India campaign in August of 1942. In London, the government began promising India dominion status. This change would put the country in the same category as Canada, Australia, New Zealand and South Africa. Civil disobedience in the Quit India campaign led to thousands of Congress members being imprisoned, including Gandhi and his deputy Jawaharlal Nehru.

When Japan conquered Malaya and Burma, it established the Indian National Army (INA) led by Subhas Bose. Most members were Indian soldiers captured in fighting. They were promised independence if India fell to Japan.

The government of Clement Atlee in London bowed to the inevitable when the war ended. It agreed to grant India self-government and dominion status by June of 1948. Former wartime military commander Lord Louis Mountbatten was appointed viceroy to oversee the process.

The Muslim-Hindu problem remained a major stumbling block. The Muslim League proposed separate Muslim states. Congress opposed this. With the problem unresolved, it was decided to split India into

Mohandas Gandhi, universally known as the Mahatma.

two separate dominions, India and Pakistan. India would occupy the center of the subcontinent while Pakistan would have two regions, east and west. East Pakistan comprised much of Bengal in the northeast. Kashmir, in the northwest, was claimed by both India and Pakistan. The dispute was left unresolved.

Partitioning provoked a mass migration of sixteen million people. Muslims in India moved to Pakistan, Hindus did the reverse. Friction between the two groups exploded into conflict. Half a million people were killed during this time.

Setting fishing nets at Goa.

India

Travelling by bicycle taxi at Trivalore.

Nehru became prime minister of India. Jinnah was governor-general of Pakistan. Dominion status came earlier than expected, on August 15, 1947. The bloodshed begun during partition continued. Gandhi was assassinated on January 30, 1948 by a Hindu extremist.

Princely states were given the opportunity to remain independent or to join India. Most agreed to join. Hyderabad held out until forced to join in 1948.

Kashmir's ruler opted to join India in 1947. He was Hindu whereas most Kashmiris were Muslim. War erupted between India and Pakistan for control. Under the terms of a 1949 cease-fire agreement, Kashmir was divided into Indian and Pakistani areas.

Dominion status was terminated in 1950. Under its new constitution, India became a parliamentary federal republic. Practical power remained in the hands of the prime minister and his cabinet. The president's role was largely ceremonial.

France's small settlement at Pondicherry was annexed by the Indian government in 1956. The Portuguese enclave at Goa was annexed in late 1960.

Nehru's India followed a policy of non-alignment in world affairs. It walked a fine line between the Soviet Union and western nations. Disputes with China over the northeastern border erupted into war in 1962. Chinese forces invaded the border region, defeating Indian troops and taking some

Indian territory. A cease-fire was declared in November.

Pakistan launched a military assault to seize India's portion of Kashmir in 1965. They were repelled and the Soviet Union sponsored cease-fire talks in 1966. The result was a return to the previous division.

Indian prime minister Shastri died while in Tashkent. His successor was Nehru's daughter, Indira Gandhi. The Congress Party split in two. Gandhi and her supporters formed New Congress. Under the slogan 'Abolish Poverty', she won a resounding victory at the 1971 elections.

East Pakistan's long-running demands for autonomy from West Pakistan were supported by India. When war broke out between east and west in late 1971, India's army intervened on East Pakistan's side. The West Pakistan army was defeated within two weeks. India had helped develop Bangladesh, the former East Pakistan.

India joined the ranks of nuclear powers in 1974. A device was detonated under the Thar Desert. There was considerable concern in western nations over this development. Some feared that India might employ nuclear weapons against Pakistan.

Mass demonstrations against her government led Gandhi to declare a state of emergency in 1975. She postponed the 1976 elections and suspended civil liberties. Gandhi suffered a major defeat in the delayed elections of 1977. The Janata Party, led by Moraji Desai, won power, but only briefly. Gandhi had regained office by January of 1980, leading the new Congress (Indira) Party.

Sikhs in Punjab were agitating for their own state by 1982. Militants began a terrorism campaign. The army responded with force, escalating the conflict. It climaxed with the army storming the Golden Temple at

Street scene in Jaipur.

An array of locally grown fruit for sale at a street stall.

Amritsar, the Sikhs' most holy place.

Gandhi was assassinated by two of her Sikh bodyguards on October 31, 1984, in retaliation. Anti-Sikh rioting exploded across the country. The party elected her son Rajiv to the leadership. He pursued a program of reconciliation with the Sikhs and won the 1984 elections decisively.

Gandhi sent troops to Sri Lanka in 1987 when Tamil separatist guerillas rebelled. They were seeking autonomy. A peace agreement was signed a few months later, but violence continued. Gandhi did not want their activities to spread to India. Troops remained in Sri Lanka until 1990.

Gandhi was defeated in 1989 by a National Front coalition

led by V. P. Singh. When a new election was called in 1991, it was expected that Gandhi would win. Before the election, Gandhi was assassinated by a Tamil separatist suicide bomber. The election was postponed for four months. Narasimha Rao became the new prime minister.

Rao made some profound changes. He began dismantling India's central planning system in favor of a market economy. Trade barriers were lowered and foreign investment encouraged.

Religious conflict continued. A Hindu mob, encouraged by the Bharatiya Janata Party, demolished the Babri mosque at Ayodhya in December of 1992. Rioting and communal violence followed, weakening Rao's government. A scandal occurred, in which members

India

of the Rao government were implicated. This further weakened his government.

Support for Rao collapsed at the 1996 elections. A United Front coalition was formed, with H. D. Deve Gowda as prime minister. It held power until early 1998. The Bharatiya Janata party gained power with support of other parties at that time. Atal Bihari Vajpayee became prime minister.

India had voted against the U.N. Comprehensive Test Ban Treaty in 1996. India detonated three underground nuclear explosions in May of 1998. The United States and Japan imposed economic sanctions in response. Pakistan escalated tensions by staging its own nuclear test. Indian forces were called in to handle Muslim guerrillas in the Indian part of Kashmir in 1999. Despite peace talks, relations with Pakistan did not improve.

India had long been the victim of terrorist attacks. When terrorists attacked New York and Washington, D.C. in September of 2001, India quickly showed its support. The U. S. lifted its sanctions against both India and Pakistan in hope of gaining cooperation in fighting terrorism.

Muslim terrorists, supported by Pakistan, bombed the Kash-

mir parliament in October of 2001. Two months later they launched a similar assault on the Indian parliament. About 750,000 Indian troops massed on the border with Pakistan, threatening an invasion by mid-2002. Pakistan backed

down and suppressed the terrorist groups. The United States sent top national security officials in to mediate the dispute. Tension between the two countries remains high as intermittent actions by terrorists continue.

An impressive example of Mughal architecture at Agra.

Indonesia

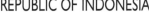

REPUBLIC OF INDONESIA

Indonesia, in Southeast Asia, is the largest archipelago in the world, comprising more than 13,600 islands, almost half of which are inhabited. The islands stretch across about 3,200 miles (5,150 km) of sea at the equator. They range from tiny tropical atolls to the large expanses of Java, Borneo and Sumatra. Much of the larger islands is coastal plains, rising to mountains of considerable height in the center. More than a hundred of these mountains are volcanic. Java has the best farmland.

Indonesia is hot all year round. The dry season occurs during the eastern monsoon from June to October. The western monsoon, from December to March, sweeps down from Asia bringing heavy rains. Volcanic eruptions, earthquakes and tsunami are occasional natural threats.

Most Indonesians are of mixed Malay background. This breaks down into well-defined ethnic groups such as the Javanese, Sundanese, Madurese, Balinese, Acehnese and Bataks. Several million Chinese and other Asians also live in Indonesia.

Indonesia is the fourth most populus nation on Earth. Nearly ninety percent of its people are Muslims. Christianity is practiced by eight percent of the population. Most of its Hindus live on Bali.

The official language is Bahasa Indonesia. This language includes elements of Dutch, Chinese, Indian and English. Many people also speak English.

Indonesia was an agricultural economy for most of the Dutch colonial era. There was little heavy industry. The government began developing manufacturing industries in the 1960s. The goal was to diversity the economy so that successful agriculture alone was not so essential to the country's prosperity.

The most profitable exports are petroleum and natural gas. Rich fields in Sumatra, Java and Borneo make it one of the major oil producers of the world. Indonesia is a major producer of rubber, sugar cane, tobacco, coffee, tea, palm oil, cacao and spices. Mineral resources include nickel, coal, manganese, gold, silver, bauxite and tin.

Indonesia harvests large amounts of teak, sandalwood, camphor and ebony. About fifty percent of the world's tropical hardwoods come from Indonesia. Almost all forest land is state-owned, so exploitation is going on with mimimal controls.

Manufacturing in Indonesia was affected by global economic problems of 1997–98, yet it continues to prosper. Principal products include textiles, clothing, footwear, chemical

Indonesia

SCOTT BRODIE

The roundabout on Jalan M H Thamrin in the center of Jakarta.

The first Indonesians were migrants from China 5,000 years ago. Indian traders arrived 3,000 years later, bringing their culture, Hinduism and Buddhism, as well as a writing system. Two types of kingdoms had grown up by the seventh century A. D. Some were based on rice farming while others focused on maritime trade.

The Hindu and Buddhist kingdoms in Central and East Sumatra were farming-based. These kingdoms left evidence of their cultures in some magnificent temples and artifacts.

The Sri Vijaya kingdom was a major maritime trading kingdom on Sumatra. It was the center of trade with Indian and China for some 500 years. Unlike the Hindu and Buddhist cultures, the Sri Vijaya left few relics of the daily life and work of its people.

When Sri Vijaya's King Kertanegara was assassinated in a court uprising, he was replaced by his son-in-law Wijaya. As King Kertarajasa Jayawardhana, Wijaya founded the Majapahit empire. By the late fourteenth century, Majapahit controlled most of what is now Indonesia.

Islam was well established on Sumatra by the late thirteenth century, having been introduced by Arab traders. The kingdom of Pasai installed Islam as its official religion in 1297. Smaller states converted to Islam to escape the Hindu Majapahit's dominance.

The Majapahit empire had crumbled into a collection of small independent states by the end of the fifteenth century. These states were in almost constant conflict with one another. Many Hindus migrated to the island of Bali.

Seeking the spices that grew in abundance, the Portugese arrived in 1511. They established a string of trading posts in what they called the East Indies. The Portugese were followed by the Dutch and the British. The Portuguese had been driven from all locations except eastern Timor by the early 1600s.

Dutch merchants founded the Dutch East Indies Company in 1602. The Netherlands government authorized it to negotiate treaties and wage war, if necessary. The company established its first trading post at Gresik. A government structure was established by 1609, with a governor-general and an advisory council.

The British East India Company established a fort in northwestern Sumatra in 1601. Many more posts were built in various places during the next several years. The British were determined to take control of trade away from the Dutch. In many cases, Dutch and local forces expelled them.

fertilizer, tires and electronic equipment.

The president is both head of state and head of government, elected for an unlimited number of five-year terms. The Majelis Permusyawaratan Rakyat (MPR), the People's Consultative Assembly, elects the president. The People's Consultive Assembly is made up of the legislature plus two hundred representatives of regional groups. Most of the members of the Dewan Perwakilan Rakyat (DPR), Indonesia's legislature, are elected by the people.

A new Dutch government revoked the Dutch East India's charter in 1799. Poor management had led the company to bankruptcy. The Dutch government now exerted direct, ruthless control over the people of the East Indies. Borders of kingdoms and territories were ignored and many local cultures were destroyed.

Dutch governors-general forced European standards and culture on the archipelago. Locals were recruited to work on public works projects. Peasants had to devote a portion of their land for export farming designed to benefit the Dutch government.

British troops occupied Java during the Napoleonic Wars, beginning in 1811. Both the Dutch and British attemped to overhaul local government

with little success. The British abandoned the area in 1814.

The Dutch tightened their economic control of the archipelago. The East Indies were contributing one-third of the finances of the Netherlands government by the mid-nineteenth century. Much of this income was used to support that country's industrialization. Farmers were forced to concentrate on crops such as coffee, sugar and spices, at the expense of the rice needed to feed the locals. Famine resulted from widespread crop failures in Java in 1845.

The opening of the Suez Canal in 1869 made Aceh, on northwestern Sumatra, of much greater strategic importance. The Dutch were determined to take control of the region, but the fiercely independent

Acehnese resisted. Although the Dutch eventually gained some control, it was never absolute.

The Hindus of Bali refused to accept Dutch control. A large Dutch invasion force landed at Sanur and naval ships bombarded Denpasar in 1906. When the Raja of Bandung led his people in a suicide march on Dutch fortifications, almost 4,000 were killed.

Following decades of agitation, the East Indies finally secured a limited parliament, called the Volksraad. It met for the first time in 1918. The members, made of Indonesians and Dutch immigrants, were elected by local councils.

Henricius (Henk) Sneevliet established the Indies Social Democratic Movement (ISDV) on May 9, 1914. It exploited friction between Dutch colonists and the Indonesian-dominated unions. A successful strike of railway workers in 1923 inspired many thousands to join the ISDV. It became the Communist Party of Indonesia (PKI) in 1925. Another independence movement, the Indonesian Students' Association (PMI), was formed in 1922.

Achmed Sukarno founded the Indonesian National Party (PNI) in 1927. The Dutch came

A home on one of the many rivers in Kalimantan on the island of Borneo.

Indonesia

Worshippers gather at a mosque at Toba.

Independence leaders agreed to participate in a Japanese-controlled government, hoping it would lead to independence.

Sukarno declared independence on August 17, 1945, shortly after Japan surrendered to the Allies. The new Republic of Indonesia came into being twelve days later with Sukarno as President and Muhammad Hatta as Vice-President. The Dutch refused to recognize the new nation.

British troops arrived in late September to maintain law and order until the Dutch returned. There were demonstrations in favor of the republic all through September and October. International pressure was put on the Dutch to grant independence. A conference in the Netherlands agreed to the new republic in the fall of 1949. The Dutch retained control of western New Guinea.

The Republic of the United States of Indonesia was declared on December 27, 1949. A new constitution was adopted. The capital was renamed Jakarta. More than 300,000 Dutch expatriates left the country. In some cases, the loss of Dutch expertise caused economic hardship.

Some regions demanded more autonomy. They felt that the politics and development of Indonesia was too centered on Java. Following military coups in 1956 and 1957, Sukarno called for a new constitution giving the president more power. He appointed a new parliament and began his Guided Democracy.

Control of Netherlands New Guinea was handed over to the United Nations, which then passed it to Indonesia in 1963. A contested 1969 referendum in the territory produced a 'yes' vote to join Indonesia formally. It became known as Irian Jaya, and has more recently been renamed West Papua.

Malaysia was created in 1963, by a combination of the British colonies Sabah, Sarawak, Malay and Singapore. Sukarno launched his Confrontation campaign in opposition to this union. Indonesian guerrilla forces infiltrated Sarawak and Sabah, clashing with British and Australian forces.

Sukarno worked to balance power between the military and the Communists (Partai Komunis Indonesia or PKI). He aligned Indonesia with China and withdrew from the United Nations on January 1, 1965. Six generals were kidnapped and murdered during a coup d'état by PKI-supporting officers on September 30, 1965. General Suharto, leader of the army's strategic command, suppressed the coup.

to fear this group as much as it did the communists. Sukarno was arrested, tried for subversion and sentenced to four years imprisonment in 1929.

Japan controlled much of Kalimantan, Sulawesi and Ambon by the end of January 1942. Air raids on Java began in early February. They took the capital city of Batavia on March 5, 1942. Japan cracked down on all political activity.

Sukarno was forced to hand over power to Suharto by 1966.

Army units and some Muslim groups began killing Communists and their supporters. Between 300,000 and one million people were killed.

Typical Indonesian architecture at Bukit Tinggi.

A new regime was established. Suharto became president in 1967. He returned Indonesia to the U.N. and reinstated ties with Western nations. Indonesia was a founding member of the Association of South-East Asian Nations (ASEAN) in 1966.

Civil liberties did not improve under Suharto, but the economy grew remarkably. Foreign investment poured in. Indonesia became notorious for corruption in government and business as Suharto consolidated his power.

Indonesia's growth came crashing to a halt in October 1997. The nation's banking system became seriously threatened as its currency plummeted in value. Indonesia was forced to seek help from foreign lenders.

The International Monetary Fund (IMF) organized a U.S.$40 billion aid package, but Suharto was reluctant to follow the strict economic measures demanded. Riots began as food prices spiralled upward. Suharto resigned the presidency in favor of his deputy, B. J. Habibie, in 1998.

Habibie agreed to a U. N. referendum in which the East Timorese could vote for independence. Violence by pro-Indonesia activists following the referendum was brought

under control a U. N. peace-keeping force. Habibie was harshly criticized for his policy. Timor became independent in May of 2002.

One remarkable figure to emerge during Habibe's presidency was Megawati Sukarnoputri, daughter of former President Sukarno. Her Democratic Party of Struggle captured thirty-four percent of the vote in the June 1999 elections.

The National Awakening Party leader, Abdurrahman Wahid, was elected President and Megawati became Vice-President on October 21, 1999. Wahed's most pressing task was to increase civilian control of the government while dimishing that of the military.

Wahid faced constant criticism from the Parliament. He was censured for his role in two corruption scandals in February of 2001. Although cleared of wrongdoing, the legislature voted to remove him from office. Wahid resigned on July 23, 2001. Megawati was immediately sworn is as Indonesia's first female president.

Terrorists exploded a series of bombs in the nightclub district of Kuta on the island of Bali in October of 2002. Close to 200 people died in the blasts, including many Australian tourists. Subsequent investigations have revealed the attack was linked to fundamentalist religious groups.

Iran

ISLAMIC REPUBLIC OF IRAN

Iran is in southwest Asia, bordered on the north by Armenia, Azerbaijan, Turkmenistan, and the Caspian Sea, on the east by Afghanistan and Pakistran, on the south by the Gulf of Oman and the Persian Gulf and on the west by Iraq and Turkey. It is dominated by a vast central plateau. The Elburz Mountain Range parallels the Caspian Sea on the north. The narrow Caspian coastal plain is covered with rich soil. Two deserts, the Dasht-e-Lut and the Dasht-e-Kavir, cover much of central Iran. Climate varies from the extreme heat of the south to the extreme cold of the Elburz Mountains. Except for the Caspian plain, Iraq gets very little rainfall.

About half of Iran's population is made up of Persians. Azerbaijanis account for twenty-five percent of the total. Minorities include the Gilakis, Mazandaranis, Arabs, Balochis and Kurds. The indigenous Luri people inhabit the western mountains.

Most Iranians are Shi'ite Muslims. The Kurd and Arab minorities are Sunni. The official language is Farsi, or Persian. It is spoken by only about half the population. The rest speak Kurdish, Baluchi, Luri or various Turkic languages.

Iran's economy is heavily dependent upon the petrolem industry. It is one of the key members of the Organization of Petroleum Exporting Countries (OPEC). The major oil fields are in Khuzestan, in the southwest, near the Persian Gulf. More than 85% of Iran's exports earnings come from petroleum products.

Natural gas is also found in abundance. Minerals such as iron, copper, lead, zinc, coal and chromite are mined largely

The bazaar at Shiraz.

in the Zagros and Elburz mountains. Extraction and refining processes are performed by state-owned enterprises.

Farms are located in the Caspian Sea area, as well as in parts of the west and south. Crops include wheat, potatoes, rice, corn, barley, cotton, beet sugar, hemp, fruits and dates. Manufactured products include textiles, rugs, processed foods, electronics, and motor vehicles.

The constitution of 1979 created a republic governed under Islamic legal principles. The head of state, the velayat faqih (supreme leader) is appointed by a religious advisory board called the Council of Guardians. The president, as head of government, is elected by the people for four years.

Collecting rose petals at Esfahan.

The legislative branch is the Majlis, or Islamic Consultative Assembly, which is also elected by popular vote.

A village-based lifestyle evolved in present-day Iran around 4000 B.C. Aryans moved into the region 2000 years later. They evolved into two groups, the Persians and the Medes. They were reunited in the sixth century B.C. by Cyrus the Great, founder of the Persian Empire. His successors expanded the empire west to Turkey and Egypt, creating a golden age of Persian civilization.

Alexander the Great conquered the region in 331 B.C. Following his death, it was broken up among his generals. They were replaced in the third century B.C. by the Parthian Empire. Six centuries later the Sassanids conquered Persia.

Conflict with the Byzantine Empire led to the Sassanids' decline and defeat by Arab invaders in 641 A.D. The region was first ruled from Medina and later from Damascus and Baghdad. The new Arab rulers introduced Islam. From then until the sixteenth century, Persia was overrun several times, first by Turks, then by Mongols under Genghis Khan, other Mongols under Tamerlane and finally by Turkomans.

GOVERNMENT
Website www.president.ir
Capital Tehran
Type of government Republic
Voting Universal adult suffrage
Head of state
Leader of the Islamic Revolution
Head of government President
Constitution 1979, revised 1989
Legislature
Unicameral Islamic Consultative Assembly (Majles-e-Shura-ye-Eslami)
Judiciary Supreme Court
Member of IMF, OPEC, UN, UNESCO, UNHCR, WHO

LAND AND PEOPLE
Land area 636,296 sq mi (1,648,000 sq km)
Highest point
Mt. Damavand 18,605 ft (5,671 m)
Coastline 1,520 mi (2,440 km)
Population 66,622,704
Major cities and populations
Tehran 6.9 million
Mashhad 2.0 million
Esfahan 1.3 million
Tabriz 1.2 million
Ethnic groups
Persian 51%, Azerbaijani 24%, Giliki/Mazandarani 8%, Kurd 7%, Arab 3%, others 8%
Religions Islam 98%, others 2%
Languages
Farsi (official), numerous others

ECONOMIC
Currency Rial
Industry
petroleum, petrochemicals, textiles, cement, construction materials, food processing, sugar refining, metal fabrication, armaments
Agriculture
wheat, rice, grains, beet sugar, fruits, nuts, cotton, dairy, wool
Natural resources
petroleum, natural gas, coal, chromium, copper, iron ore, lead, manganese, zinc, sulphur

Iran

Shah Ismail established the Safavid dynasty in 1502. He restored the old boundaries of Persia and brought stability to the region. The Shi'ite Muslim faith became the state religion. Shah Abbas, ruler from 1587 to 1629, established relations with Britain. He expelled Portuguese traders who had set up along the gulf coastline.

Afghanistan invaded in 1722 and held Persia for fourteen years. They were driven out by Nadir Shah who founded the Afshar dynasty. His despotic rule ended with his assassination in 1747. His successor, Karim Khan, presided over a period of peace during which Shiraz became the capital.

Aga Muhammad Khan founded the Qajar dynasty in 1794. Although widely hated, his dynasty lasted until 1925. During this time Britain gained increasing control over Persia's trade and finances.

The discovery of oil in 1900 provoked a competition between Russia and Britain for control of Persia. The weakened Qajar dynasty made a number of concessions to both countries. It also permitted the establishment of a national assembly in 1906.

The Anglo-Russian agreement of 1907 divided Persia into three zones. The north was Russian-influenced and the south British-influenced. In the center was a neutral buffer zone. There followed a coup d'état and a long period of unstable government.

In 1914 British commercial interests took control of the Anglo-Persian Oil Company. The country was occupied by Russian and British forces during World War I. Britain claimed a protectorate over all of Persia in 1919. Russian responded by establishing the Soviet Republic of Gilan in the north.

The situation was resolved in 1921 when Colonel Riza Khan staged a coup. He established a military dictatorship with himself as prime minister. Five years later he was elected Riza Shah Pahlavi by the Majlis. He began a program of industrialization and modernization. He reduced Islam's influence on government at the same time. He renamed the country Iran in 1935.

The United States, Great Britain, Germany, Turkey and the USSR all tried unsuccessfully to form an alliance with Iran during World War II. Both Great Britain and the USSR occupied Iran's oil fields in 1941. They expelled all Axis interests from the country. Shah abdicated in favor of his son, Muhammad Riza.

St Thaddeus church is the main pilgrimage center for Armenian Christians in Iran.

LONELY PLANET IMAGES – PAT YALE

LONELY PLANET IMAGES – JOHN BORTHWICK

Schoolgirls in Tehran.

Muhammad Riza was more than willing to cooperate with the Allied powers. The U. S., Great Britain, and the USSR made extensive improvements in Iran's transportation to aid in transporting military supplies to the USSR's fighting front in 1943. When the war ended, the Soviets wanted to develop an oil industry within Iran. Iran announced a plan to develop its own oil industry, hoping for U. S. aid. The United States made a $26 million loan to Iran for the purchase of surplus American army equipment.

Prime Minister Mohammed Mossadegh came to power in 1951. He nationalized the Anglo-Persian Oil Company against the wishes of the Shah. A subsequent British blockade of Iranian ports brought the oil industry to the point of collapse. The Shah removed Mossadegh but he regained power in 1952, forcing the Shah to flee the country.

With covert support from the United States and European powers, pro-monarchists deposed Mossadegh in 1953. The Shah returned and an agreement was reached for British, French, Dutch and American companies to jointly operate Iran's oil facilities.

The Shah launched the White Revolution, a program of social and economic modernization in 1963. Large family-owned estates were purchased, divided and sold off to the people. More than one million former tenants had become landowners within three years. The right to vote was extended to adult women.

Such positive moves were offset by the oppressive measures used by the Shah to retain power. His liberalizations were opposed by the Islamic clergy. Their leader, Ayatollah Khomeini, was expelled from Iran in 1964. SAVAK, the secret police force created in 1957, became notorious for its brutal methods of suppressing opposition.

Britain withdrew its forces from the region in 1971. The Shah greatly increased Iran's defense budget with support from the United States. This was a strategic move to prevent greater Soviet influence in the region.

OPEC nations imposed an oil embargo on the United States, Europe and Japan in 1973. Iran declined to participate, but it did enthusiastically push oil prices to unheard-of levels. The resulting revenue boom was used to further modernize the country and strengthen the armed forces.

The extravagant lifestyle of the Shah and the vast wealth of a minority of the population created deep resentment in the rest of the population. This exploded into strikes and massive anti-Shah demonstrations in 1978. The loudest call was for the return of Ayatollah Khomeini.

Iran

The situation deteriorated, prompting the Shah to declare martial law in September. Chaos continued. The Shah fled Iran on January 16, 1979.

Khomeini flew to Iran from Paris to overthrow the last vestiges of the Shah's administration. A new constitution was adopted. While the president was head of state, Khomeini remained the ultimate authority. Strict Islamic standards were reimposed. Western values were banned and women were forced to adopt traditional veiled dress. Many key industries were nationalized.

Violence increased as various religious factions fought for control. One group seized the United States embassy in Tehran in November, taking sixty-six hostages. Thirteen were soon released but Iran had demands for the release of the other fifty-three.

An economic boycott failed, as did a military rescue mission. The crisis lasted until 1980, when the United States agreed to ends its freeze on U.S.$8 billion of Iranian assets.

Control of the Shatt al-Arab waterway, at the head of the Persian Gulf, had long been disputed by Iran and Iraq. It turned to open warfare when Iraq invaded Iran on September 22, 1980. Although the Iraqis were initially successful, Iran's large armed forces retaliated, bringing the invasion to a halt.

Up to one million people were killed or injured during the six-year war. The Iranians used suicide attacks by vast waves of soldiers. The Iraqis responded with horrendous chemical weapons. The war extended to the Persian Gulf in 1984, with attacks on oil tankers and U.S. Navy vessels protecting them. Iran and Iraq finally agreed to a cease-fire in August of 1988.

Attempts were made to rebuild the economy and increase the flow of oil to the west once the war had ended. Khomeini's death in 1989 enabled a relaxation of the hard-line attitude towards Europe and the United States. President Ali Akbar Rafsanjani had normalized relations with many European nations by the late 1990s. U. S. Secretary of State Madeleine Albright acknowledged U. S. mistakes in past dealings with Iran. She called for a "new season" in U. S. - Iran relations.

The U. S. launched an assault on Afghanistan's Taliban regime following the September 11, 2001, attacks on New York and Washington. Iran offered to aid in missions to rescue U. S. pilots. It also offered its ports as shipping centers for relief supplies to Afghanistan. The United States continues trade and investment sanctions. President George W. Bush described Iran as part of an 'axis of evil', linking it with Iraq and North Korea in 2002, prior to the war against Iraq.

The ruins of Darius Palace at Persepolis.

Iraq

REPUBLIC OF IRAQ

Most of Iraq, which is located in western Asia, is flat, low-lying desert. It is crossed by two great rivers, the Tigris and the Euphrates. The rivers converge at the Persian Gulf. Between them is a wide, low plain where most of Iraq's farming takes place. Mountains make up much of the far northern and northeastern areas. Most of Iraq's rain falls between the rivers and in the mountainous northeast. The temperature ranges between hot summers and cool winters in central Iraq. Temperatures in the mountains can be very cold.

Arabs make up eighty percent of Iraq's population. Kurds, who live in the northeast, are the next largest group. Islam is the state religion. Around sixty percent are Shi'ite, while the balance, including the Kurds, are Sunni. Arabic is the official language.

Iraq's economy was severely crippled after the 1990–91 Gulf War. Oil, from the vast northeastern fields, previously accounted for ninety-five percent of the nation's revenue. Imposition of United Nations sanctions has reduced the output by two-thirds.

Income from Iraq's textile, chemical, and electronics industries is small. Crops include wheat, tomatoes, barley, rice, a variety of fruits, and cotton. Iraq is one of the largest producers of dates in the world.

Prior to April of 2003, Iraq was controlled by the Regional Command of the Arab Ba'ath Socialist Party. Following the invasion of Iraq in March by the United States and Great Britain, the government of Saddam Hussein was destroyed. A new Iraqi government has yet to be formed.

The region of Iraq was the cradle of some of the world's earliest civilizations. The Sumerian civilization arose sometime before 3000 B. C. and was well-established during the next two thousand years. The Sumerians were conquered by the Persian Empire under Cyrus the Great in the sixth century B.C. Persian control lasted until the conquest by Alexander the Great in 331 B.C. Alexander's successors held the region, known as Mesopotamia, until 27 B.C. They regularly repelled Roman attempts to add Mesopotamia to its empire.

Mesopotamia was absorbed into the Sassanian Empire in the second century A.D. Arabian forces swept into the region to depose the Sassanians in 637. With them came the Islamic faith. Mesopotamia was controlled from Damascus until 750. The Abbasids established a capital at Baghdad when they took power. During their reign the Shi'ite sect became predominant. Baghdad grew into a cen-

Iraq

ter of great learning and artistic expression under the Abbasids.

The Mongols all but destroyed Abbasid culture in the thirteenth century. This was followed by periods of Turkmen and Persian control. The Ottoman Empire began exerting power over Mesopotamia in 1534. By the nineteenth century, the region was administered as three provinces, Basra, Mosul and Baghdad. Considerable social and economic advances were-made during this time.

The Ottomans were allied with Germany in World War I. British forces invaded southern Mesopotamia in 1914 and occupied Baghdad by 1917. Independence movements grew, aided by British Col. T. E. Lawrence, otherwise known as Lawrence of Arabia. The country was not initially granted independence, but was to remain under British protection.

An Arab Council of State was established after an independence revolt was suppressed by British forces in 1920. Faisal al-Husein became King Faisal I of Iraq in August of 1921. A 1924 treaty gave Britain the right of veto over the Council's legislation and permitted British military bases on Iraqi soil. Iraq joined the League of Nations in 1932 as a

sovereign state. British control was formally ended at that time.

Iraq signed an agreement with the Iraq Petroleum Company for development of oil fields in the Mosul region in 1931. This internationally owned company built pipelines across Iraq and paid royalties to the Iraqi government. These funds as well as additional royalties from new oil fields discovered in the 1950s were used to fund national development.

Iraq, responding to its treaty of alliance with Britain, severed relations with Axis powers at the outbreak of World War II. Premier Nuri as-Said, the pro-British leader, was overthrown in 1940. Arab nationalist Rashid Ali al-Gailani became premier

of a new pro-Axis government. British forces landed in Iraq and defeated the new government within thirty days. A new pro-Allies government was established.

When Syria and Egypt merged as the United Arab Republic (UAR) in February 1958, Iraq reacted by uniting with Jordan to form the Arab Union. Nuri al-Said was named its premier. The UAR, outraged at this new union, encouraged Iraqis to overthrow their gov-ernerment. Iraqi General Karim Kassam led a military coup on July 14th, 1958. Said and King Faisal, the crown prince, were assassinated.

Kassem declared Iraq an Islamic republic and the Arab Union dissolved. Iraq laid claim

Ali El Hadi Mosque at Samarra.

LONELY PLANET IMAGES – JANE SWEENEY

**United Nations weapons
inspectors in Iraq
during 1992.**

to the whole of Kuwait and to
Iranian territory near the Persian Gulf.

Kurds in the northeast, led
by Mustafa al-Barzani, revolted
against Iraqi rule in 1962. Seeking an independent Kurdistan,
they captured a large part of
northern Iraq. Their position
was compromised when the
Shah of Iran withdrew his support in 1975.

Political friction resulted in
another coup in February 1963.
Right-wing military officers and
members of the Ba'ath movement took power. They began a
bloody purge of rebels throughout the country. The Ba'athists
were removed from govern-
ment by another coup in late

1963. Yet another coup, this
time led by Major-General
Ahmad Hasan al-Bakr, brought
them back to power again in
1968.

Until this time Iraq had
maintained good relations with
the United States which provided it with economic and military aid. An Arab-Israeli war
in 1967 altered this relationship. The United States supported Israel in this conflict.
Iraq, in turn, closed off its oil
pipeline to Western nations.
Iraq began fostering stronger
relations with the Soviet Union.
It nationalized the Iraq Petroleum Company in 1972, thus
increasing its own oil profits.

Al-Bakr was replaced as president by Saddam Hussein
Takriti on July 16, 1979. Ten
days later an unsuccessful coup
was launched. Hussein began

purging the Ba'ath movement
of his opponents.

With tensions over owner-
ship of the Shatt al-Arab at
breaking point, Iraq invaded
Iran in 1980. Initially Iraqi
forces made good advances
against the Iranians. However,
Iran quickly regrouped and
began pushing the invaders
back. The conflict bogged
down into an eight-year conflict. There were more than one
million people killed or injured.
A United Nations-sponsored
cease-fire took effect in August
of 1988.

Saddam Hussein revived a
dispute with Kuwait, on Iraq's
southeastern border, in 1990.
Iraq had long claimed Kuwait
as part of its territory. Hussein
claimed Kuwait was exceeding
OPEC oil production quotas and
thus pushing down the interna-

Iraq

A billboard in suburban Baghdad promotes President Saddam Hussein.

tional price of oil. This was reducing Iraq's oil revenue, desperately needed to pay for the long war with Iran. Hussein demanded compensation but Kuwait refused.

More than 100,000 Iraqi troops invaded Kuwait on August 2, 1990. The country fell quickly. Soon Iraqi forces were massed along the border with Saudi Arabia. The United Nations applied vast economic sanctions against Iraq but Hussein refused to withdraw.

A U.S.-led military coalition was assembled with U.N. authorization. Air attacks began the campaign on January 16, 1991. The huge force quickly pushed the Iraqis out of Kuwait. As part of the terms for ending the war, Iraq was to permit United Nations inspectors to check for nuclear or chemical weapons. Evidence was found of a capacity for producing both.

Coalition aircraft attacked targets in Iraq in 1993 when the cease-fire terms were breached. In May of 1996 the U.N. agreed to limited sales of oil for the purchase of direly needed food and medicines.

Iraq made efforts to limit the activities of United Nations weapons inspectors in late 1997. This provoked air raids against suspected weapons facilities by

coalition forces. Inspectors were permitted back into Iraq.

U. S. president George W. Bush declared Iraq part of an "axis of evil" with Iran and North Korea in early 2002. Bush made it clear that he wanted to remove Saddam Hussein from power. The U.N. Security Council proposed new weapons inspections in Iraq. After months of negotiation, inspections began in November of 2002. Inspectors found 12 warheads designed to carry chemical weapons. Reports filed soon after suggested a belligerence and lack of real cooperation on the part of Hussein's government.

On March 19, 2003, the United States began air strikes

against Iraq's leadership in Baghdad. Forces led by the United States and Britain continued an assault on the government of Saddam Hussein. On April 15, President Bush announced that the regime of Saddam Hussein had been destroyed. U.S. and British forces have remained in Iraq for peacekeeping purposes. In the months following the official end of major hostilities on April 15, the main focus of the U.S. and British forces was to continue the search for weapons of mass destruction, further the reconstruction of the country and formation of a new government, and battle sporadic armed resistance by Iraqis.

Ireland

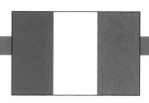

REPUBLIC OF IRELAND

GOVERNMENT
Website www.irlgov.ie
Capital Dublin
Type of government Republic
Independence from Britain
December 6, 1921 (dominion status)
Voting Universal adult suffrage
Head of state President
Head of government Prime Minister
Constitution 1937
Legislature
Bicameral Parliament (Oireachtas)
House of Representatives (Dail Eireann), Senate (Seanad Eireann)
Judiciary Supreme Court
Member of CE, EU, IMF, OECD, UN, UNESCO, UNHCR, WHO, WTO

LAND AND PEOPLE
Land area 27,136 sq mi (70,283 sq km)
Highest point Carrauntoohill 3,373 ft (1,041 m)
Coastline 4,692 mi (1,448 km)
Population 3,883,159
Major cities and populations
Dublin 1,300,000
Cork 275,000
Limerick 105,000
Ethnic groups Irish
Religion Christianity
Languages
Irish, English (both official)

ECONOMIC
Currency Euro
Industry
food products, brewing, textiles, clothing, services, mining, chemicals, pharmaceuticals, machinery, glass, software
Agriculture
turnips, barley, potatoes, beet sugar, wheat; beef, dairy
Natural resources
zinc, lead, natural gas, barite, copper, gypsum, limestone, dolomite, peat, silver

The Republic of Ireland occupies about eighty percent of the island immediately to the west of Great Britain. The rest of the island is Northern Ireland, which is part of the United Kingdom. Ireland's landscape is attractive rolling country, punctuated by lakes and rivers. The central plain is ringed by low mountains in the north, west and south. The western mountains create a rugged coastline against the Atlantic Ocean. Ireland's climate is temperate, with cool winters and warm summers. Heavy rainfall contributes substantially to the fertility of the landscape.

Ireland is known for the vast numbers of its people who have migrated to other countries, notably the United States, Canada, Britain and Australia. Most Irish people are descended from Celts who conquered the island in the third century B.C.

About ninety-five percent of the people are Catholic. English and Irish are both official languages. Most people speak English. Irish (Gaelic) is commonly spoken in the western areas.

Ireland was predominantly an agricultural economy until recent years. The mass emigration of its population was a huge drain on resources. Recent, persistent efforts to build a service- and manufacturing-based economy have

proved highly successful. Government incentives encouraged corporations to establish diverse manufacturing plants and service industries. Tourism is also a key factor in the economy. The economy boomed in the late 1990s. Unemployment remains high, however, in the 2000s.

The president is elected by the people for a seven-year term as Ireland's head of state. The prime minister, nominated by the lower house of the legislature and appointed by the president, is head of state. A cabinet called the Council of State is approved by the lower house and selected by the prime minister. The bicameral parliament is known as the Oireachtas. The lower house is the Daíl Éireann (House of Representatives) and the upper house the Senead Éireann (Senate).

In prehistoric times Ireland's people had a similar lineage to those of Britain. Celtic tribes arrived around 300 B.C. The island was colonized by the Milesians, Tuatha De Danann, Firbolgs and Fomors. Neither the Romans nor the Saxons, both of whom conquered Britain, crossed the channel to Ireland.

Christianity was introduced around A.D. 430, largely through the efforts of St. Patrick. Paganism remained

Ireland

popular until the end of the fifth century.

Tribes developed different provinces, each ruled by a king. These kings followed a high king called Meath, based at Tara. The provinces were frequently at war with one another. Many monasteries built during this time became centers for learning and art.

Ireland's first emigration came in the fifth century when groups of its people crossed to Scotland. The next major upheaval came in the eighth century with the arrival of Viking invaders. They established settlements along the eastern coast, notably Dublin, Limerick and Waterford.

The warring kingdoms were unable to mount any serious opposition to the Vikings. Brian Boru became high king in 1002 and set about uniting the kingdoms. The Irish finally expelled the Norse invaders at Clontarf in 1014. The unity did not last and wars between the kingdoms resumed.

Pope Adrian IV authorized England's King Henry II to take control of Ireland in the twelfth century. The English soon established themselves in Dublin and other towns on the east coast. The Irish put up strong resistance to many inva-

The Customs House on the banks of the River Liffey in Dublin.

sions for more than one hundred years. The British finally prevailed. Use of the Irish language and marriage between English and Irish people were forbidden.

Edward Bruce of Scotland invaded in 1315, gaining strong Irish support. The English were pushed back into an enclave around Dublin known as the Pale. Other conflicts diverted England's attention until the late fifteenth century. Sir Edward Poynings forced Ireland's parliament to pass legislation in 1495 making it completely subservient to England.

When King Henry VIII broke away from the Catholic Church in 1537, he had Irish monasteries closed. He wanted to neutralize any threat from Catholic Ireland. His Church of Ireland, however, made little headway against Catholicism. Three Irish rebellions were brutally suppressed during the reign of Queen Elizabeth I.

Confiscated Irish lands in the northeast were given to Protestant settlers from Scotland by King James I. A major rebellion, begun in 1641, was crushed in 1650 by English forces led by Oliver Cromwell. Hundreds of thousands of lives were lost.

Catholic King James II of England was overthrown in 1688 and replaced by Protestant William III of Orange. Irish patriots rallied to support James, provoking the first large-scale clash between Protestants and Catholics. Forces led by James clashed with William's army at the Battle of the Boyne near Dublin in 1690. The defeat of Catholic forces left a legacy of bitterness which permeates Irish society to this day.

Citizenship and the right to own property were stripped from Irish Catholics. Control of the country went to the Protestants, who were known as the Ascendancy. Large-scale emigration began at this time. Many Irish departed for the new American colonies.

The American Revolution and agitation from Irish Protestants led to some reforms. The independence of Ireland's parliament was restored and trade concessions granted in the 1780s. Wolfe Tone, a Protestant, formed the Society of United Irishmen which staged a rebellion in 1798, aided by France.

British Prime Minister William Pitt conceived the United Kingdom of Great Britain and Ireland as a way of avoiding more rebellions. The Irish parliament was abolished and Irish Protestants were given representation in Britain's parliament under the 1800 Act of Union. Pitt's plans for Catholic emancipation were stymied for many years. Irish Catholics were finally included in the Westminster parliament in 1829.

Further independence moves were abandoned in

The ruins of Dunbrody Abbey, near Waterford, testify to Ireland's long religious history.

BRAND X PICTURES

Ireland

the 1840s. A failed potato crop led to widespread starvation. Another large-scale migration to North America and Australia followed. Ireland's population dropped by almost two million between 1845 and 1851.

The gulf between Catholics and Protestants widened in the following decades. Industrialization helped the Protestant north to prosper, while the agricultural south struggled. The Young Ireland movement and the more militant Sinn Féin began pushing for independence. Groups pressured Britain to grant Ireland its own parliament. The home-rule movement was successful in 1914.

Protestants in Northern Ireland opposed home rule as it threatened their supremacy. The Irish Republican Brotherhood, led by Patrick Pearse and James Connolly, staged an uprising in Dublin on Easter Monday of 1916. British troops eventually put down the rebellion and executed the leaders.

Sinn Féin won 73 of the 106 Irish seats in the 1918 British elections. They declared a mandate to create a republic and Ireland's own parliament. Sinn Féin was banned by Britain as a result. Irish insurgents, later known as the Irish Republican Army (IRA) began attacks on government establishments. Britain dispatched troops to reinforce the Irish police. Known as the 'black and tans',

for the color of their uniforms, they were widely despised for their brutality.

Britain established a parliament for Ulster in Protestant Northern Ireland in December of 1920. The Anglo-Irish Treaty of 1921 created the Irish Free State, a self-governing dominion

BRAND X PICTURES

with the same status as Canada and other countries.

Sinn Féin, led by Eamonn de Valera, opposed the Irish Free State concept, preferring a republic. Civil war broke out between opposing groups. De Valera led his Fianna Fáil party to power in the parliament in 1932. He became prime minister, gradually severing his ties to the IRA. He wrote a new constitution in 1937 for an independent Ireland. Ireland became a republic in 1948.

Violence between Catholics and Protestants in Northern Ireland increased in the 1960s. All citizens were forced to surrender their firearms. The Republic of Ireland was admitted to full membership in the European Economic Community (EEC) in 1973. From this time on Ireland's economic fortunes began to turn around. The establishment of new industries brought unprecedented prosperity by the late 1990s.

The IRA announced that it would begin disarming in October of 2001. British Prime Minister Tony Blair responded by declaring that 13,000 British troops would be removed from Northern Ireland. Further moves toward a lasting peace have been made since that time.

An ancient windmill used for milling grain in County Wicklow.

Israel

STATE OF ISRAEL

Located in southwestern Asia, Israel is on the east end of the Mediterranean Sea. Excluding the occupied West Bank areas, it is a narrow, irregularly shaped region. Nearest the Mediterranean coast are the the Plain of Zevulun, the Plain of Sharon and the Plain of Judea. Most of Israel's large cities and industry are in this area. The Jordan River runs north and south from the Lebanon-Syrian border to Lake Tiberias (the Sea of Galilee), east of these plains. It flows on to the Dead Sea, which lies at approximately 1,296 feet (395 m) below sea level. This is the lowest surface area on Earth. The hills of Galilee dominate the north, while the Negev Desert covers most of the south. Northern Israel enjoys a Mediterranean climate with warm summers and cool winters. The Negev Desert has hot, dry, summers and cold winters.

Israel is highly urbanized. Over ninety percent of its people live in cities and towns. Eighty percent of the people are Jewish, most of whom migrated there after Israel was founded in 1948. The original arrivals were from Europe, particularly after World War II. This was followed by a flow of Jews from countries such as Iraq and Syria. After the Soviet Union collapsed, large-scale immigration from Russia began. There is also a small population of Ethiopian Jews called Falashas. About seventeen percent of the people are Arabs.

Most of the Jewish majority are either Ashkenazim or Sephardim. Other smaller groups include the Falashas, Samaritans and Karaites. Most of the Muslim population is Sunni. Christians and Druses make up a very small minority.

Hebrew and Arabic are the country's official languages. While Hebrew is more commonly used, Arabic is spoken by at least seventeen percent of the people. Arabic is also used in schools, legal affairs, and the legislature. Many people also speak English.

Israel was created from the British mandated territory of Palestine in 1948. The region was home to the Canaanites some time before 2000 B.C. They developed an alphabet from which other writing systems evolved. Their religion had a major influence on Judaism, Christianity and Islam.

Various invaders challenged the Canaanites during the next several hundred years. A confederation of Hebrew tribes called the Israelites took control about 1125 B.C. Their king, David, established a capital at Jerusalem. Palestine fell to Assyria in 721 B.C. and was conquered by Babylonia in 586 B.C.

Israel

The Persians, Greeks and Romans all conquered the region at various times. Rome established the semi-autonomous state ruled by Jewish kings in 63 B.C. Christianity was established from the teachings of Jesus Christ during the Roman period. It dominated until Arabs conquered the region in A.D. 638 and began to convert it to Islam.

Crusaders conquered the region in the name of Christianity in the eleventh century A.D. They were expelled by the Muslim military commander Salah al-Din in 1187. Palestine fell to the Turkish Ottoman Empire in the sixteenth century. It remained under Ottoman rule until 1918.

Theodore Hertzl founded the Zionist movement in the late nineteenth century in Europe. It promoted the large-scale movement of Jews from all over Europe to Palestine. Jewish immigration to Palestine greatly increased. Jews revived the Hebrew language and founded Tel Aviv in 1909. Anti-Zionist groups had formed among Arab Palestinians by 1914.

The Ottomans allied with Germany and Austria–Hungary in World War I. Britain recruited both Arab and Jewish

Contrasting architecture in Tel Aviv.

guerrilla fighters to harass the Turks. Britain's Balfour Declaration of November 1917 supported the principle of a Jewish national homeland in Palestine, providing the rights of non-Jewish communities were protected.

Jewish immigration increased when the League of Nations gave Palestine to Britain as a mandated territory in 1922. Violent clashes between Arabs and Jews in 1929 prompted Britain to consider restricting Jewish immigration.

The Zionists believed Britain favored the Arabs. Guerrilla units from both sides clashed repeatedly and the death toll rose. British troops were caught in the middle. A revolt by Arabs in 1936 evolved into a major campaign against the Zionists. Almost a quarter of a million Jews arrived in Palestine from 1933 to 1939.

As details of the Nazi Holocaust emerged, Zionists escalated their campaign for a Jewish homeland. Britain refused to admit 100,000 Holocaust survivors, but many entered illegally.

In 1947, the United Nations proposed a division of Palestine into a Jewish state and an Arab state. Jerusalem and Bethlehem would be part of an international zone. The Zionists agreed but the Arab League refused. Unable to achieve a

solution, Britain withdrew from Palestine. The State of Israel was proclaimed with its capital at Tel Aviv on May 14, 1948.

The Arab League attacked Israel almost immediately. Forces from Syria, Egypt, Lebanon, Iraq and Transjordan attempted to conquer Israel. Their failure resulted in Israel acquiring more land than originally granted by the United Nations. Large numbers of Palestinian Arabs became refugees.

Israel's government was headed by Prime Minister David Ben Gurion. Chaim Weizmann was president. Large-scale immigration of Jews from all over Europe began in earnest. Armistice agreements were signed with the Arab League nations. The Gaza Strip on the Egypt-Israel border was left under Egyptian occupation, while the West Bank was annexed to Jordan.

Israeli military units invaded Egypt's Sinai Peninsula in 1956. The plan was to seize control of the Suez Canal from the Nasser government of Egypt. The plan collapsed when the United States refused to support it.

Egypt made guerrilla raids into Israeli territory for many years. It mobilized troops for a major assault in May of 1967. Israel sent its army into Egypt's

Performing a bar mitzvah at the Western Wall in Jerusalem.

FLAT EARTH PICTURE GALLERY

Sinai region and into Syria's Golan Heights on June 5th. The Egyptians and Syrians were crushed in six days. The Israeli army pushed through to the Suez Canal. Israel now controlled the Sinai, the west bank of the Jordan River, the Arab section of Jerusalem and the Golan Heights. It was more than three times the size it had been before the war.

Terrorist attacks were made against Israel by guerilla groups within the Palestine Liberation Organization (PLO). Then, on October 6, 1973, the Jewish holy day of Yom Kippur, Egypt attacked Israeli forces in the Sinai. Syria attacked those in the Golan Heights at the same

Israel

time. The Arabs received substantial backing from the USSR, Saudi Arabia and Kuwait. Oil-producing nations cut off petroleum exports to the U. S. and other Western nations because they had aided Israel. The Israeli economy suffered a huge setback.

A United Nations-sponsored cease-fire became effective in late October. U.S. Secretary of State Henry Kissinger had negotiated Israel's withdrawal from the Sinai and the Golan Heights by 1974. Beginning under the leadership of Menachim Begin in 1977, Israelis were encouraged to settle in the occupied territories.

Egyptian leader Anwar Sadat began peace talks with Israel that same year. This led to the Camp David Accord in March of 1979. Egypt recognized the state of Israel and Israel returned the Sinai to Egypt.

The position of Palestinian Arabs continued to trouble Israel. The Palestine Liberation Organization, headed by Yasser Arafat, sought a separate Palestinian state. The PLO's guerrilla campaigns led Israel to invade Lebanon in 1982. Israel sought to eradicate the PLO, which was headquartered in Beirut, Lebanon. Palestinians staged an uprising, called the Intifada, against Israelis in the late 1980s. The result was many deaths and ongoing terrorist activities.

Iraq launched missiles against Israel during the Gulf War in 1991, in an attempt to provoke Israel into retaliation.

Yitzhak Rabin of the Labor Party became prime minister in 1992. Peace talks were staged between the PLO and Israel the following year. The result was limited self-rule for the Palestinians in the Gaza Strip and Jericho, with self-rule in the West Bank region to follow.

A treaty with Jordan was concluded in 1994, ending a 46-year war between the two nations. Rabin was assassinated in November 1995 by a right-wing Israeli opposed to the West Bank accord. Benjamin Netanyahu was elected prime minister the following year.

Netanyahu continued negotiations with PLO leader Yasser Arafat regarding the withdrawal of Israel from the Hebron region. Ehud Barak, Netanyahu's successor in 1999, signed a new timetable with Arafat for troop withdrawal.

Palestinian militants began a new wave of suicide bombings, killing large numbers of Israeli civilians. PLO leadership appeared unable to control the militants. Israel, under Prime Minister Ariel Sharon, launched violent assaults on the Palestinian areas during 2002, drawing widespread criticism. In 2003, negotiations began in earnest between Israelis and Palestinians to end the bloodshed and plan a Palestinian state.

The Dome of the Rock in Jerusalem is holy to both Judaism and Islam.

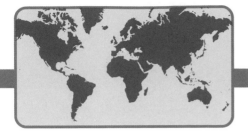

Italy

ITALIAN REPUBLIC

Italy lies on the Mediterranean Sea in southern Europe. More than half of the country consists of the Italian peninsula, which extends into the sea from the continental mainland. It also comprises the islands of Elba, Sicily and Sardinia, plus many lesser islands. Contained within its borders are the independent enclaves of the Vatican and San Marino. The far north is dominated by the Alps, while the fertile Lombardy Plains lie south of the mountains. Along the spine of the peninsula is the Appenine mountain range. It extends the full length of the country and continues on to Sicily. The River Po is the dominant waterway of the north. Its tributaries in the highlands form a number of major lakes. The southern regions have experienced occasional serious earthquakes.

Italy's climate varies from north to south. The north is predominantly temperate, with warm summers and cool winters. The region nearest the Adriatic Sea tends to be colder because of prevailing northerly winds. Southern regions enjoy a Mediterranean climate, with mild winters and hot summers. Sicily is sub-tropical.

About seventy percent of Italians live in urban areas. Nearly all of the people are of Italian descent. Large numbers of refugees fled into Italy from the former communist countries of Eastern Europe in the 1990s. Most Italians are Catholic, but there are small Jewish and Muslim minorities. Italian is the language of the overwhelming majority.

Italy has developed into a substantial industrial nation since the 1950s. Most manufacturing is centered in the north around Genoa, Turin and Milan. The main products are iron, steel, motor vehicles, machinery, chemicals, electrical equipment, textiles and clothing. Until recently certain key strategic industries were state-owned, but a program of

The highly atmospheric canals of Venice.

SCOTT ERODIE

Italy

privatization was carried out in the 1990s.

Agriculture dominated Italy's economy until World War II. Half the total land area is presently devoted to crops or pastures, particularly in the fertile north. Beet sugar, tomatoes, potatoes, corn, soybean, olives, wheat and other grains are the principal crops. Olive oil is produced on a large scale from locally grown olives. Grape growing is widespread, catering to the Italian wine industry.

Mining is limited. Oil is found in Sicily, while iron ore, bauxite, sulphur, lignite, marble and mercury are mined on the mainland. Abundant natural gas resources are being utilized. The mountainous northern regions are ideal for the pro-duction of hydroelectric energy.

The current constitution of Italy came into effect in 1948. The parliament is bicameral. Members of the lower house, the Chamber of Deputies, are elected by the people. Representatives from twenty regional parliaments elect members of the Senate (the upper house). The head of state, a largely ceremonial role, is the president. Presidents are elected at a joint session of both houses of parliament. The prime minister and the council of ministers govern the country with the support of the Chamber of Deputies. Each of Italy's twenty regions has its own parliament. Ninety-four provinces make up the regions.

The Forum in Rome was the heart of the Roman Empire.

There is little written history of Italy before 500 B.C. The Ligurian people appear to have been its original inhabitants. Etruscans migrated south into Italy from Asia Minor around 800 B.C., quickly gaining dominance over the Ligurians. Greeks also established settlements on the Gulf of Taranto in the eighth century B.C. Most had gone into decline by the fifth century B.C.

Celts invaded the northern Po River region in the fourth century B.C. They quickly overcame Etruscan opposition, driving most of them south. The Etruscans were opposed by Greeks as they headed south.

Along the western coast, the Latin and Sabine civilizations escaped the Etruscan encroachment.

According to legend, the city of Rome was established by Romulus in 753 B.C. The lowlands of Latium suffered from severe malaria. Rome, being built on higher ground, overcame this problem. Etruscans infiltrated the region and came to dominate everyday life in Rome.

The last Etruscan king was overthrown in about 510 B.C. Rome became a republic, governed by two elite patricians elected by the people. Eventually the people elected members from their own ranks as tribunes. The Senate gathered more and more power until it effectively controlled the republic by the third century B.C.

The Romans built the Servian Wall around the city about 310 B. C., following a Celtic invasion. Rome began conquering nearby regions at first. Rome controlled most of central and southern Italy by 279 B.C. It occupied the island of Sicily by the third century B.C.

Growing more ambitious, Rome provoked a conflict with the Carthaginian Empire of northern Africa. Their battles in the Punic Wars left Carthage broken and Rome triumphant. Greece, Macedonia and Egypt were all under Roman control by the mid-second century B.C.

Widespread corruption in Rome was responsible for the gradual demise of its democratic institutions. Julius Caesar was dictator of the empire by 48 B.C. He conquered Gaul (France) and various other regions. Rome controlled all of

Italy, parts of north Africa, Egypt, Palestine, Syria, Gaul, Spain and parts of the Balkans by the time of Caesar's assassination in 44 B.C.

Octavian came to power in the chaos after Julius Caesar's assassination. He defeated a challenge to his rule by Marc Antony and Queen Cleopatra at Actium in 31 B.C. The Senate gave him the title Augustus as a reward. He became emperor of Rome.

Augustus laid the groundwork for two hundred years of peace and prosperity. He divided Italy into eleven administrative regions. As well as commercial and military success, there was a great flowering of art and literature. Much of England was brought under Roman control during the reign of Emperor Claudius from A.D. 41-54. Emperor Nero rebuilt Rome with new and spectacular buildings and superior roads, following the great fire in A.D. 64.

The religious movement begun in Palestine by Jesus Christ had spread to Rome by this time. Roman emperors were considered divine, but Christians acknowledged only God as divine. Such a flagrant challenge to the emperors' authority led to brutal persecution. Despite the best efforts to

The red-tiled roofs of the town of Lucca.

Italy

The famous leaning Tower of Pisa.

accelerated rapidly after this time.

Visigoth invaders swept down from the north to sack Rome in 410. The last western emperor was Romulus Augustus. He ruled for two years from 474. Although his empire collapsed, the eastern emperors maintained a claim on the territory. The Ostrogoth leader, Theodoric the Great, invaded Italy in 493. A period of relative stability followed.

The east was now known as the Byzantine Empire. Under the leadership of Justinian I and his wife Theodora, it conquered Italy in the mid sixth century. The Lombards had deposed the Byzantines in most parts of Italy by 569. Only Rome resisted Lombard dominance.

The Lombards were preparing to take Rome in 751. Pope Stephen II appealed to King Pepin the Short, ruler of the Franks, for help. Although most of Pepin's domain lay in France, his son, Charlemagne, routed the Lombards. As a result, Pope Leo III crowned Charlemagne Emperor of the West in 800.

Power in Italy passed mostly to local rulers. The authority of the popes declined markedly. Otto I of Germany deposed King Berengar II in 961 after an

appeal from the pope for protection. He was named Holy Roman Emperor as a reward.

Northern Italy had been successfully plundered by Magyar invaders prior to this time. In the south Arabs had conquered Sicily and by 917 were threatening the mainland. The Holy Roman Empire controlled Germany and Italy, in theory at least. Their dominion over Italy was never more than tenuous.

The Normans, from northwestern France, captured Sicily from the Arabs in the eleventh century. They also gained control of Apulia and Calabria on the mainland. They established a strong feudal system. The Kingdom of Naples was created under their control.

Over succeeding years, the history of the north was marked by the rise of the city-states. Their strength developed from commercial interests banding together for protection against land-owning nobles. The most prominent of the city-states were Venice, Florence, Milan and Genoa.

The Lombard League was formed in the twelfth century to repel attempts by Emperor Frederick I to control the city-states. Battles in the thirteenth century led to the development of opposing factions in the league. The nobles formed the Ghibellines while the cities united as the Guelphs. Their conflicts led to the collapse of

crush it, Christianity grew and flourished across the Roman Empire. Emperor Constantine, who ruled from 306 to 337, became a Christian and legitimized the new faith.

The Roman Empire began a long decline at the end of the second century A.D. In 284 Emperor Diocletian divided it into four sections, two eastern and two western. Constantine moved the capital to Byzantium, renaming it Constantinople. It later became Istanbul.

The empire was permanently divided into east and west in 395, with the eastern empire based in Constantinople. The western emperor, Honorius, moved the capital from Rome to Ravenna. The decline of the Roman Empire

The ancient port city of Genoa, located in north-western Italy.

Wars. Pope Julius united the regions around Rome. They were known as the Papal States. He failed to achieve the wider unity which would have protected Italy against invaders.

The Italian Wars ended in 1559 with Habsburg Spain controlling Naples and Milan, and dominating the papacy in Rome. Following the 1701-14 War of the Spanish Succession, Spain's Italian territories passed to the Austrian Habsburgs. The city-states declined markedly as northern and western Europe rose to dominance.

Military leader Napoleon Bonaparte of France launched a major military campaign in 1796 which swept the Austrians from power. Italy was reconstructed under his control. He made extensive land reforms and created new republics.

The north became the Italian Republic very briefly. Napoleon changed it to the Kingdom of Italy in 1805. He

imperial rule and the rise of papal control.

The great city-states encouraged arts and literature. Botticelli, Da Vinci and Michelangelo all rose to prominence. Marco Polo set out from Venice on his epic crossing of Asia during the thirteenth century. The city-states were economically exhausted by decades of fighting by the end of the fifteenth century.

France and Spain were locked in a battle to control parts of Europe at this point in time. France's invasion of Italy in 1494 sparked the Italian

Carnival time in Venice.

Italy

became monarch. Regions as far south as the Rome-based Papal States were under French control by 1812.

The Congress of Vienna restored Italy to most of its pre-Napoleonic state when he was defeated in 1815. The Austrians once more took control, provoking a resurgence of nationalism.

The Risorgimento, or unification movement, sought to re-unify Italy and end constant fighting between the various regions. The radicals wanted a republic, the liberals sought a union dominated by the House of Savoy, while Catholic conservatives promoted a federation led by the pope.

The leader of the Risorgimento was Giuseppe Mazzini, a radical. He established a repub-lic based in Rome in 1849, but Pope Pius IX called in French troops to crush the movement.

The King of Piedmont, Victor Emmanuel II, committed his army to support France in the 1854-56 Crimean War. When France won the Franco-Austrian War in 1859, Austria ceded Lombardy, in northern Italy, to France. France then handed it to Piedmont in exchange for Nice, Parma, Savoy and Modena.

The King of Piedmont united Tuscany and some of the Papal States in 1860. Giuseppi Garibaldi's army captured Sicily and Naples in 1861, incorporating them with Piedmont. With much of the land integrated, Victor Emmanuel II became King of Italy in March of 1861.

The region of Venetia was secured from Prussia in 1866, following its war with Austria. The French protectorate over the Papal States ended in 1870. When the pope refused to relinquish control of Rome to the king, Italian troops occupied the city and declared it the capital of Italy. The new alliance held. Representative government was introduced under under King Humbert I between 1878 and 1900.

Italy sought to be a colonial power in Africa at the end of the nineteenth century. It conquered parts of Somaliland in 1889 and Eritrea in 1890. Attempts to do the same in

The ancient Temple of Concordia on Sicily.

BRAND X PICTURES

The Colosseum — the massive landmark in the centre of Rome — was built in the heyday of the Roman Empire

Ethiopia were thwarted by fierce Ethiopian resistance in 1896.

Italy joined the Allied powers during World War I. Its forces won a major victory at Vittorio Veneto in 1918. The end of the war saw the breakup of the Austro-Hungarian Empire. As one of the victorious Allies, Italy secured new territory in South Tyrol, Trieste, Carniola, Istria and the Dalmatian Islands.

The settlement was less than Italy had been promised when it entered the war. The most disappointing aspect was the country's failure to gain control of the Adriatic coast of Yugoslavia. Subsequent national dissatisfaction encouraged the rise of the Fascist Party, which had been founded in 1919 by Benito Mussolini and others.

The growth of communism, both in Italy and internationally, aided the Fascists whose increasing popularity led to a threat to storm Rome if they were not given power. King Victor Emmanuel III, bowing to pressure, asked Mussolini to form a government in October 1922. This coalition lasted two years.

Socialist leader Giacomo Matteoti was assassinated in 1924. Mussolini used this as an excuse to suspend parliament and adopt dictatorial powers. He concluded the Lateran Treaties with the pope in 1929, ceding control of Vatican City in Rome to the Catholic Church.

A new assault was launched on Ethiopia in 1935. This time Italy was successful in conquering the country. Ethiopia was

incorporated with Eritrea and Somaliland to become Italian West Africa. International condemnation prompted Italy to resign from the League of Nations in 1937.

Mussolini entered into a treaty with Hitler's Germany in 1936. He also provided aid to the Fascist General Franco in the 1936-39 Spanish Civil War. Tens of thousands of Italian troops were sent to to Spain under the guise of being civilian volunteers. All political parties other than the Fascists were banned in 1938. Italian expansionism led to the conquest of Albania in 1939.

Italy supported Germany, but it did not enter World War II until France fell in 1940. Most Italian forces remained in north Africa after war was declared. This was an attempt to overwhelm British forces in Egypt. A huge Allied offensive in 1940-41 saw thousands of Italians taken prisoner. Germany's Afrika Corps was deployed to replace the failed Italian effort.

Allied forces had landed in Italy by 1943. Its major industrial cities and ports were under constant bombardment. The king dismissed and imprisoned Mussolini in July, and

Italy

appointed Pietro Badoglio in his place. The following month Italy surrendered to the Allies. German forces immediately occupied northern Italy.

A German commando raid freed Mussolini, who established a puppet regime in the north under German control. Mussolini was captured and executed by Italian partisans in April of 1945.

Anti-fascist groups formed a coalition government during 1945, with Christian Democrat Alcide de Gasperi as prime minister. King Victor Emmanuel III abdicated in May 1946, to be succeeded by his son, Humbert II. Italians narrowly voted in favor of a republic in a referendum the following month. The monarchy was terminated, ending Humbert's short reign.

A new republican constitution was adopted on January 1,1948. Italy became a member of the North Atlantic Treaty Organization (NATO) the following year. It joined the United Nations in 1955.

Italian politics in the postwar years is largely a history of unstable coalitions. Most were engineered to prevent the communists from gaining control of the national government. Communists did, how-

A view across the main lagoon in Venice.

Florence's historic Ponte Vecchio.

SCOTT BRODIE

ever, have major successes in regional and local governments.

Despite this political instability, Italy's social and economic development was spectacular. The pre-war agricultural nation was transformed into one of western Europe's major industrial powers. This prosperity brought growing trade union strength and militancy. Strikes and other disruptions became regular events.

Control of the government was intermittently conservative and liberal. By the mid-1970s the economy had become increasingly chaotic. Corruption and organized crime had become commonplace in many areas. The left-wing Red Brigade terrorist group kidnapped former prime minister Aldo Moro in 1978. His subsequent murder outraged the nation.

The Socialists became dominant in government for the first time in 1983. Their leader, Bettino Craxi, held power for four years. This was a remarkably difficult period in Italian politics. Wages were cut, taxes increased and social services

reduced in a bid to bring order to the economy. The Catholic Church lost its status as the state religion during his tenure. Two brief administrations by Christian Democrats followed. Disputes within that party made effective government difficult for its leaders.

Socialist leader Giuliano Amato became prime minister in 1992. He launched major austerity measures to deal with inflation and the national debt. High unemployment, corruption among government officials and fear of pervasive Mafia involvement led to widespread discontent. The proportional representation voting system, which was the cause of Italy's unstable governments, ended in 1993.

Industrialist Silvio Berlusconi became prime minister in March of 1994. He led a coalition of neo-fascists and conser-

vatives which collapsed in December. Six years of rapidly changing coalition governments followed, led by Lamberto Dini, Romano Prodi, Massimo D'Alema and finally Giuliano Amato.

Berlusconi's conservative coalition was given a solid mandate by voters in the 2001 elections. His administration has been plagued by accusations of conflicts of interest. Berlusconi's myriad business interests include much of Italy's commercial television sector. As prime minister he has considerable influence over the state-owned broadcasting network. Following the 2001 attacks against the U. S., Berlusconi vowed to make his country a partner in the war against terrorism. Berlusconi offered Italy's troops as well as the use of its ports and airports.

Jamaica

The third largest island of the Greater Antilles of the West Indies in the Caribbean Sea, Jamaica is located directly south of Cuba. Most of the island is a limestone plateau, with the heavily forested Blue Mountains in the east. The coastal fringe is heavily cultivated. Hot springs are found in various parts of Jamaica. The island is subject to serious earthquakes. The climate of Jamaica is tropical with fairly consistent temperatures throughout the year.

Seventy-five percent of the population is descended from African slaves. Fifteen percent are African-European. There are European and Indian minorities. Most people are Protestant Christians, although spiritualist cults and sects such as Rastafarianism are popular. English is the official language, but many people speak a Creole dialect which includes elements of African and European languages. The economy of Jamaica is based on agriculture, mining, manufacturing and tourism.

Arawak peoples, who migrated to the island around 700 A.D., named it Xaymaca, meaning land of springs. A small Spanish settlement was established in 1509 at Saint Iago de la Vega (now Spanish Town). The settlers brought brought diseases which wiped out most of the Arawaks.

Britain captured the island in 1655, taking formal control in 1670. Slaves were brought from Africa to work the sugar plantations. Jamaica became a major producer of sugar and cacao. Port Royal, the chief slave trading center, prospered hugely until an earthquake swept it into the sea in 1692.

Former slaves staged an uprising at Morant Bay in 1865 in protest to discrimination. The government imposed martial law and the insurrection ws suppressed. Jamaica became a crown colony the following year. A massive earthquake in 1907 killed nearly 1000 people and damaged buildings in the capital city of Kingston.

Universal adult suffrage was granted in 1938. The first election was held in 1944. Jamaica joined other British Caribbean colonies to form the Federation of the West Indies in 1958. The federation failed. Jamaica declared independence on August 6, 1962. Alexander Bustamente was prime minister.

The next decades saw intermittent governments under either the People's National Party or the Jamaican Labor Party. Hurricane Gilbert caused $8 billion in damage and left 500,000 people homeless in 1988. Various reforms have brought continual slow economic growth despite a serious slump of the mid-1990s.

GOVERNMENT
Website www.cabinet.gov.jm
Capital Kingston
Type of government
Parliamentary democracy
Independence from Britain
August 6, 1962
Voting Universal adult suffrage
Head of state
British Crown,
represented by Governor-General
Head of government Prime Minister
Constitution 1962
Legislature
Bicameral Parliament
House of Representatives (lower house), Senate (upper house)
Judiciary Supreme Court
Member of Caricom, CN, IMF, OAS, UN, UNESCO, WHO, WTO

LAND AND PEOPLE
Land area 4,244 sq mi
(10,991 sq km)
Highest point
Blue Mountain Peak
7,402 ft (2,256 m)
Coastline 635 mi (1,022 km)
Population 2,680,029
Major cities and populations
Kingston 650 000
Spanish Town 98,000
Portmore 92,000
Ethnic groups African 75%,
African-European 15%, Indian 4%,
Religions Christianity 81%,
Rastafarian 9%, spiritualism 10%
Language
English (official)

ECONOMIC
Currency Jamaica dollar
Industry
tourism, bauxite, textiles, food processing, light manufactures, rum, cement, chemicals, sugar refining
Agriculture
sugar cane, bananas, coffee, citrus, potatoes, vegetables, poultry, dairy
Natural resources
bauxite, gypsum, limestone

Japan

Japan comprises four main islands — Honshu, Hokkaido, Shikoku and Kyushu — plus many smaller islands, including Okinawa to the south. The landscape is very beautiful, with deep valleys and soaring mountains, and numerous waterways and lakes. The most extensive plains are located on the island of Hokkaido. Many of the mountains, which extend across the islands from north to south, are volcanic. Earthquakes are extremely common. The main island of Honshu has a wide eastern coastal plain. In the center is Mount Fuji, Japan's tallest peak.

Winters are cold, with winds from the Asian mainland blowing snow across most of the islands. By contrast, Pacific winds make summers warm and often very humid. Rainfall is usually heavy through most of the year. Typhoons often sweep in from the surrounding oceans.

The Tokyo-Yokohama region, on the island Honshu, is the most populous on Earth. About three-quarters of Japan's people live in metropolitan areas. Japanese is the official language, but English is often used in business.

Most of the people have Japanese heritage. The only significant non-Japanese groups are Koreans and a tiny number of Ainu people on the island of Hokkaido. Koreans and Ainu together amount to less than one percent of the population.

Most Japanese are adherents to both Shintoism and Buddhism. There is a small number of practicing Christians. Shinto evolved from ancient times and is the indigenous religion of Japan. Many traditions and aspects of Japanese culture have some relationship with Shinto. There are no sacred texts. The objects of worship are natural elements such as mountains, the sun and

Freeways are shoehorned into much of the available space in Tokyo.

SCOTT BRODIE

Japan

SCOTT BRODIE

trees. The famous Mount Fuji is considered sacred by Shinto. Ancestors and national figures may also become objects of worship.

Japan's industries were badly damaged during World War II. Reconstruction meant modern facilities which focused on heavy industry. Its industrial strength has grown steadily since that time. Japan was the leading shipbuilding country and one of the leading producers of electronics, steel and motor vehicles by the 1990s. Brands such as Nissan, Mazda, Toyota, Panasonic, Sony and Akai had become well-known around the world. It was among

Crowded streets in the Shibuya district of Tokyo.

the top producers of chemicals, textiles and synthetic fibers. Much of Japan's heavy industry is concentrated in southern Honshu island and northern Kyushu. The major industrial centers are Yokohama, Tokyo, Kobe, Nagoya and Osaka.

About forty percent of Japan's farmland is devoted to rice-growing. Other major crops include wheat, barley, potatoes, sugar beets, fruits, vegetables and tobacco. Most Japanese farms do not devote much time or acreage to raising livestock. Advanced farming methods and the best chemical fertilizers have made Japanese farms among the most productive in the world.

Japan is among the world's leading countries in the production of electricity. Its petroleum and natural gas resources are extremely limited. Nearly a quarter of Japan's total annual imports are mineral fuels.

The Japanese fishing fleet is one of the world's largest. Fish is the second most important food item next to rice. Seaweed and other marine plants are also important staples of the Japanese diet.

The constitutional monarchy of Japan dates from 1847. The emperor was considered to be divine prior to the end of World War II. Today, emperors are fig-

ureheads without any real power. The head of goverment is the premier, who represents a majority of the national legislature. That legislature, called the diet, is bicameral. The House of Representatives, or lower house, and the House of Councillors, or upper house, are both elected by the people. Representatives serve for four years, councillors for six. The premier chooses the cabinet from members of the diet at the diet's approval. Both the prime minister and the cabinet are responsible to the diet.

Archeological research has found that the Ainu arrived in Japan from Korea or Manchuria as early as 1500 B.C. They were a simple people. The Ainu engaged in fishing, hunting and some agriculture. Today only a small community remains.

Early written chronicles of Japanese history indicate that Jimmu founded the first Japanese Empire in 660 B.C. More advanced, and skilled in working with bronze and iron, these people soon overran the Ainu. They were the basis of today's Japanese society.

A system of uji (clans) had developed by the fourth century A.D. They were mainly geographically based. Uji were very hierarchical. Groups of related families took the leadership roles with a king–priest at the top.

Gradually one uji, the Yamato, gained influence over others in the central and western regions. Yamato's base was initially at Nara. This expansion occurred mostly by force and laid the groundwork for Japan's ruling structure. The Yamato leader was acknowledged as emperor. He controlled taxation, the military and other key aspects of society.

Soon there emerged the concept of the emperor as a divine being. The Yamato emperor claimed descent from Amaterasu Omikami, the sun goddess. He expected his subjects not only to obey him, but also to worship him as a god. This unyielding structure remained in place until 1945.

Early Japanese society was modelled on that of China. Yamato endeavored to put in place a centralized administration similar to that of China. Intellectuals studied and emulated all things Chinese, adapting them to Japanese uses. Japanese architecture, dress, calligraphy and arts all have roots in Chinese culture.

Buddhist priests brought their religion to Japan in about 550. At first there was a cultural clash between Buddhism and Shinto. Although Buddhism was adopted by the Yamato court as its official religion, many uji adhered to Shinto.

Yamato ruled without opposition until the mid-ninth century when the imperial court became dominated by the Fujiwara clan. Previously just one of many uji, the politically astute Fujiwara married into the ruling family. They left the emperor in place but manipulated his every action from behind the scenes, supported by Buddhist priests.

Although Fujiwara controlled the court of the emperor, they could not always impose their will on daimyo (uji leaders), particularly those far from the capital. Daimyo maintained a military force called samurai (those who serve) to protect farmers and others from harassment. The daimyo expected a share of the produce or other services in return. This was the basis of the long-lasting Japanese feudal system.

Fujiwara's strategy of intermarriage in the ruling classes produced many descendants. The more distant of these, known as Taira and Minamoto, were banished from the capital. They gained sufficient power in the provinces to eventually challenge Fujiwara. Civil war raged for most of the twelfth century as the rivals fought for control.

The Taira clan gained power in about 1160 under emperor Kiyomori. The Minamoto clan had defeated Taira in battle by 1185. Yorimoto, daimyo of Minamoto, set up a capital at Kamakura, near present-day Tokyo

Yorimoto founded a military regime, taking the title of

Pachinko gambling machines are a favorite leisure pastime in Japan.

Japan

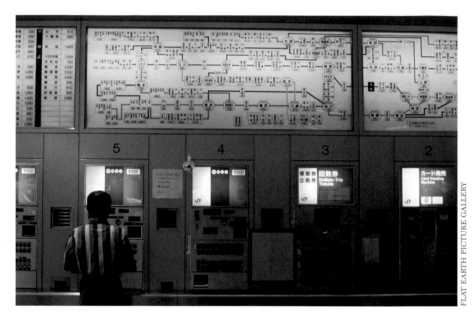

Ticket-vending machines for the Tokyo subway system.

shogun, which meant "commander-in-chief for the suppression of barbarians," in 1192. He maintained the myth that the emperor was in control. Yorimoto's heirs, who gained power upon his death in 1199, all fell to conspiracies or assassinations. The Hojo took control of the country in 1219.

The Hojo preferred to manipulate power from behind the scenes. Various Fujiwara were appointed as shogun, although under tight restraint. Hojo, whose control lasted until 1333, gave Japan a new legal system. Two invasions by Kublai Khan's Mongol forces were successfully repelled during the Hojo reign.

Constantly diverted by the prospect of another Mongol invasion, the Hojo administration became shaky. The emperor, Daigo, exploited

his popularity with the people to stage two attempts, in 1324 and 1331, to reinstate imperial rule. Sent into exile, he was replaced by one of his more compliant relatives.

Daigo returned from exile in 1333 when daimyo Ashikaga Takauiji deposed Hojo. The emperor abolished all shogu-

nates and daimyo and tried |to disperse their samurai. He sought a return to total imperial power. Takauiji's reaction was to remove Daigo from power once again.

The Ashikaga took Kyoto as their capital, with Takauiji as shogun, but failed to consolidate their power. The daimyo began fighting among themselves. Life for ordinary Japanese became chaotic as bandits roamed the countryside.

Japan had split into several autonomous regions, each under the control of a daimyo by the early 1500s. Each daimyo tried to become shogun. Oda Nobunaga of Owari province captured Kyoto and routed the Ashikaga in 1568. He killed

An electric commuter train on the vast Tokyo rail system.

thousands of Buddhist monks in the hope of ridding the country of Buddhism as a political force. His dictatorship lasted until 1582.

After Nobunaga came Toyotomi Hideyoshi, who spent much of his time reuniting the land. He ordered the samurai into castles close to the daimyo who controlled them. His rule was close to absolute by 1590. Most daimyo united behind him, either voluntarily or not. He left a five-year-old boy as his successor when he died in 1598.

Japan began developing international trade during this time. Merchant ships created links with China, Korea and Southeast Asia. Japanese seafarers also became notorious as bloodthirsty pirates preying on traders in the region.

The daimyo once more battled for control. Tokugawa Ieyasu claimed victory in 1603. His base was Kanto province, with a capital at Edo (now Tokyo).

Tokugawa allowed the other daimyo free rein in their provinces, providing they swore total allegiance to him. Those who did not found their wives and children held hostage at Edo to secure their compliance.

Tokugawa was adept at ensuring his officials never gained too much power or influence. He divided society into daimyo, samurai, peasants, artisans and merchants — a rigid class structure based on Confucian ideals.

Portuguese traders first reached Japan in 1543. Before long they were trading Chinese silk to Japan. They gladly accepted Japanese in exchange for a wide range of European goods, including guns, lacquerware and copper products. Portugal soon had well-established trading centers at Hirado and Nagasaki.

Traders were closely followed by Catholic missionaries in 1549. Francis Xavier landed on Kyushu and was soon converting people to the faith. The missionary work expanded rapidly despite opposition from Shinto and Buddhist priests.

In the late sixteenth century the Spanish arrived, planning to break Portugal's monopoly. The church was working with the merchants. Franciscan mis-

Most cities in Japan are linked by ultra-high-speed Shinkansen, also known as 'bullet trains'.

FLAT EARTH PICTURE GALLERY

Japan

sionaries wearing disguises began arriving on the first ships.

The last of the Europeans to arrive were the British in 1613. They were encouraged by a British sailor, Will Adams, who had been shipwrecked on the coast in 1600. He became a confidant of Tokugawa Ieyasu, teaching the shogun mathematics and Western-style shipbuilding.

The rise of Christianity concerned Japan's leadership as early as the 1580s. Toyotomi Hideyoshi ordered all Christian missionaries out of the country. Many disobeyed. He retaliated by executing missionaries who had been openly converting Japanese in Kyoto and Osaka in 1597.

Tokugawa Ieyasu outlawed Christianity completely in 1614. Severe persecution of Christians had become commonplace within four years.

Shogun Tokugawa Iemitsu brought a halt to all foreign arrivals in 1639. He embarked on a campaign to return the nation to values that had prevailed before the Europeans sailed into view. Japanese were forbidden to travel overseas. Only a small number of Dutch, Korean and Chinese were permitted to remain in Nagasaki to trade.

Japan remained all but closed to the outside world for 200 years. Three United States Navy ships arrived in Tokyo Bay on July 8, 1853. One was a steamship, something the Japanese had never seen before. The leader of the mission, Commodore Matthew Perry, had orders to force Japan to open ports for trade with the United States.

Perry departed when the Japanese refused to allow him to land. He returned with a well-armed fleet of eight ships on February 13, 1854. Perry's force of arms convinced the Japanese to relent. Following

Traditional Japan meets European and American commerce at Yokohama in the nineteenth century.

ELECTRA COLLECTION

FLAT EARTH PICTURE GALLERY

The Imperial Palace contrasts with the commercial buildings of Tokyo.

long negotiations the Treaty of Kanagawa was signed on March 31, 1854, giving trading rights to the United States. Soon afterwards the same concessions were granted to European powers.

There was shock and outrage that the shogun had conceded so much. Although a minority saw the chance to modernize and industrialize, most favoured expulsion of all foreigners. Attacks on foreigners brought severe retaliation: warships bombarded ports, killing many locals.

An anti-shogun group of fanatical samurai was formed by the daimyo of Chushu, Hizen, Tosa and Satsuma provinces, as well as various

nobles in the imperial court. Their plan was to depose the shogun and restore full imperial power. They were successful in 1867, when the last shogun, Hitotsubashi, resigned.

Thus began the Meiji Restoration. The under-age Emperor Mutsuhito ruled with the help of a range of advisers, Japan once more was under the control of an absolute monarch, a person considered by his subjects to be divine. The imperial capital moved from Kyoto to Edo, which was renamed Tokyo.

The feudal system was dismantled within four years. Each daimyo handed over his lands to the emperor, enabling widespread land reform.

The samurai were disarmed and released. They staged minor revolts against the emperor, all of which failed.

Compulsory military service was introduced. The Imperial Japanese Army was equipped with Western-style uniforms and armaments.

Foreign expertise was recruited to develop a modern infrastructure. Telegraphic communication was introduced. A railway line linking Tokyo with Yokohama opened in 1872. Early railways were built with British assistance, but the Japanese soon learned to continue on their own. Ships bought from Scottish shipyards were copied to establish Japan's own shipbuilding industry.

The emperor initially ignored calls for democracy, but he later tried to suppress them. Neither tactic worked. In 1880 Ito Hirobumi was directed to produce a new constitution that preserved the powers of the emperor.

Japan

A parliament of two houses, called the diet, was established in 1890. Members of the lower house were elected by the people, while upper house members were appointed by the emperor.

The restoration of imperial power brought a surge in nationalism. Japan joined the European powers in their quest for colonial domination. War was declared against China in 1894. Japan took the Pescadore Islands, Formosa (Taiwan) and the Liao Tung region in Manchuria.

Czarist Russia was expanding eastward in the early twentieth

A woman wearing traditional Japanese dress in Tokyo.

century . Supported by a pact with Britain, Japan demanded that Russia relinquish its claims to Korea. Russia refused, so Japan declared war in 1904. The world was stunned when the Japanese forces defeated the Russian navy.

Japan officially annexed Korea in 1910. It wanted to secure Korea's vast mineral deposits to feed its ever-growing industrial complex.

Japan joined the Allies against Germany and the Austro–Hungarian empire in World War II. It occupied German territory on the Shandong peninsula in China. Japan successfully demanded China give it major economic concessions in Manchuria and Inner Mongolia.

The emphasis on both colonial expansion and increased military power was curbed in the 1920s. Business interests gained more and more political power. Economic growth was temporarily halted by the devastating earthquake of 1923. It killed about 150,000 people and destroyed most of the Tokyo–Yokohama region.

Hirohito, the grandson of Emperor Meiji, ascended to the throne in 1926. His policy of Showa, or "enlightment peace," was not popular with military leaders.

The downgrading of military power led many officers to form or join secret societies. Their plan was to establish a military dictatorship. The steady growth of unionism and communism was also concerning them.

Certain military officers in Manchuria wanted to return to aggressive expansion of the country. They attacked Chinese troops near Shenyang (then known as Mukden) without the support of Tokyo. They had captured most of Manchuria by 1933.

Many Japanese supported the rebel army. They believed the Western powers were trying to destroy their country. Prime Minister Inukai

Middle-level managers, known as 'salarymen', are the backbone of Japanese business.

A typical Japanese meal.

The military took control of Japan in 1940. An admirer of Hitler, Minister for the Army General Tojo Hideki proposed a partnership with Germany and Italy. Subsequently he promoted a plan to take control of France's Indochina and the Dutch East Indies.

Tojo developed the idea of the Greater East Asia Co-Prosperity Sphere. Japan would rule and Japanese business would exploit the mineral and other wealth of the lands. Japan occupied Indochina in September of 1940. The following month Tojo became prime minister.

The United States imposed an embargo on the sale of oil, iron, rubber and steel to Japan. This only encouraged the militarists. It was now urgent that

Japan take control of Malaysia for its rubber and Borneo for its oil, they argued fervently.

Admiral Isoruko Yamamoto convinced Tojo that it was essential to destroy the U.S. Navy fleet in Hawaii. The Co-Prosperity Sphere became a reality. Six aircraft carriers dispatched their aircraft to attack military installations in Hawaii on December 7, 1941. Much of the U. S. Navy's Seventh Fleet was destroyed at its moorings.

Simultaneously, forces attacked Wake Island, Hong Kong, the Philippines and Malaysia. Territory as far south as New Guinea had been captured by the middle of 1942 . The triumphant advance was halted in the Papua New Guinean jungles and the Coral Sea, as the Allied defense began. A month later the Japanese fleet was soundly

Tsuyoshi disagreed with the army's actions. He was assassinated in May of 1932. Subsequent years saw a series of weak governments. A coup d'état staged in February 1936 was eventually put down after several ministers were assassinated.

Following a clash with Chinese troops near Beijing, the Japanese swept through northern China on July 7, 1937, capturing Nanjing, Beijing and Shanghai. Troops committed many atrocities against civilians, including bayoncting, beheading, rape and looting.

Traditional Japanese decorated paper lanterns.

Japan

The Ginza district of Tokyo, with its expensive restaurants and fashion stores.

defeated at the Battle of Midway.

The Japanese occupation of eastern Asia was marked by brutality and widespread atrocities. Local peoples and prisoners-of-war were treated barbarically. They were starved and beaten by Japanese guards in prison camps. Some were made to work as slave laborers.

Gradually, between 1942 and 1945, Allied forces pushed the Japanese back. Vast numbers of Japanese and American soldiers and marines died in horrific battles in the Pacific. Allied forces fought northward from island to island in the southern Pacific, driving out the Japanese.

The Japanese saw an immense setback with the fall of Saipan, a base in the Mariana Islands, in 1944. Tojo was forced to resign as head of the military.

The taking of Okinawa enabled the Allies to unleash a sustained bombing campaign against Japanese cities in 1945. Bombing attacks devastated Japan's communications, industry, and what was left of its military. The horror of war was brought home to the Japanese population for the first time.

Realizing an invasion of Japan would result in millions of deaths, United States President Harry Truman authorized the use of atomic bombs. The first was dropped on Hiroshima on August 6th. The second was dropped on Nagasaki on August 9th. Soviet forces had invaded Manchuria, northern Korea and Karafuto at the same time.

Japan acccepted the Allies terms of surrender on August 14, 1945. The official documents were signed aboard the USS Missouri in Tokyo Bay on September 2nd.

Dazed, the Japanese were now confronted by foreign occupation of their country. General Douglas MacArthur was made Supreme Commander, Allied Powers. The Japanese accepted the situation

peacefully because the emperor instructed them to do so.

MacArthur began a wholesale restructuring of society. Militarists were purged from the government and civil service, and the army was all but disbanded. MacArthur used Hirohito to ensure the changes were accepted. The emperor's divine status had been officially terminated.

Major land reform was instituted and the diet was fully democratized. The occupation lasted until April of 1952. Japan was admitted as a full member of the United Nations in 1956.

Japan's peaceful transformation into a world manufacturing and economic power was astounding after the war.

FLAT EARTH PICTURE GALLERY

Japanese taxis waiting for fares late at night.

Helped by large amounts of U.S. aid between 1946 and 1952, Japan embarked on a concerted program of developing selected industries.

Japanese automobiles were appearing on the streets of the world by the 1950s. Its cameras, electrical equipment and watches were gaining a reputation for quality and reliability.

Society changed too. Business adopted Western-style dress and corporate structures. Revolutionary production and management techniques were adopted with great success.

Japanese quality and value were crushing much of the Western competition by the 1970s. Corporations were building automobile factories around the world by the 1980s.

Economic growth was continuous, despite many periods of government corruption. Japan had one of the highest standards of living in the world and unemployment was almost unknown. The country's main problems were overcrowding and pollution.

An economic crunch came in the 1990s. With faltering world demand and slowing growth, many corporations were in difficulty. They began laying off thousands of employees. Corporations collapsed and the nation's inefficient banking system was closely monitored.

Junichiro Koizumi became prime minister in 2001, with strong popular support. His cabinet has diverse members, including several women. A new and more devastating economic recession has set in since that time. Incidents involving U. S. military personnel in Okinawa in 2001 have prompted renewed concern about ongoing U. S. presence in the country.

Tokyo Stock Exchange

FLAT EARTH PICTURE GALLERY

59

Jordan

HASHEMITE KINGDOM OF JORDAN

Jordan is in the far-southwestern corner of Asia. Its only coastline is a strip of land on the Gulf of Aqaba in the south. The central plateau rises abruptly from the eastern shores of the Jordan River and the Dead Sea then slopes downward to the Syrian Desert in the extreme east part of the country. The area west of the Jordan River, known as the West Bank, was formerly Jordanian territory. It is separated from Jordan by the Great Rift Valley. The Arabian Plateau in the south features mountains and deep valleys. Jordan's winters are cool, and its summers are hot and dry. Most precipitation comes in the winter months.

Almost all Jordanians are of Arab descent. There are tiny Circassian and Armenian minorities. Ninety-five percent of the people are Muslims. The majority of these are Sunni. Arabic is the official language.

The Ammonites and the kingdoms of Edom, Gilead and Moab were situated east of the Jordan River around 2000 B.C. These kingdoms were subsequently conquered by Egyptians, Assyrians, Babylonians, Persians and Romans.

Arabs seized Jordan from the Byzantine Empire during the seventh century A.D., introducing Islam. Christian Crusaders from Europe ruled Jordan in the twelfth century. It came under the control of the Turkish Ottoman Empire four hundred years later.

The Ottomans were allied with Germany in World War I. Arab nationalists joined with the British in the Arab Revolt which overthrew Turkish control. The region, called Transjordan, became a League of Nations mandated territory, under British control in 1920. Transjordan was closed to Jewish immigration.

Britain appointed Emir Abdullah ibn Hussein to head semi-autonomous Transjordan in 1923. Five years later the British gave up all but financial and foreign relations control. British General John Glubb created the Arab Legion which fought alongside the Allies in World War II.

Britain granted independence to the Hashemite Kingdom of Transjordan on May 25, 1946. It became a U.N. trust territory at that time. Transjordan troops joined in the unsuccessful Arab war against Israel in 1948. The country's name was changed to Jordan the following year. The West Bank region was annexed in 1950. Jordan inherited large numbers of Palestinians who had fled Israel in 1948. King Abdullah was assassinated in 1951. He was succeeded by his son Talal I.

The stark landscape of Jordan's Dana Valley.

FLAT EARTH PICTURE GALLERY

A police officer guarding Roman archaeological sites at Petra.

A short-lived union with Iraq was established in February 1958. The United Arab Republic (Egypt and Syria) was involved in a revolt against Iraq's goverment in July of 1958. Jordan dissolved its federation with Iraq and severed diplomatic relations with Egypt. Relations were not restored until 1964, when the Arab League pressed for unity in dealing with Israel.

Jordan joined Egypt in attacking Israel in 1967. Israel captured Jordan's West Bank region. Guerrillas supporting a Palestinian homeland fought Jordan's efforts to reclaim the territory. The conflict climaxed in a ferocious ten-day civil war in September of 1970. Jordan's prime minister was assassinated by the terrorist Black September movement in 1971. King Hussein survived an attempt on his life in late 1972.

Jordan's role in the 1973 Yom Kippur War against Israel was minor. It reluctantly recognized the Palestine Liberation Army as sole representative when it gave up claims to the Israeli-occupied West Bank region. King Hussein subsequently gave up all rights to the area in 1988.

Thousands of refugees fled to Jordan during the Persian Gulf War. A worldwide embargo on Iraq affected Jordan as well. These events did considerable damage to Jordan's economy.

In 1994 King Hussein reached a peace agreement with Israel. He began using diplomatic channels to promote relations with Israel among other Arab nations. Rioting occurred throughout the country in 1996 due to austerity measures intended to aid the economy. King Hussein died in 1999. He was replaced by his son Abdullah.

The new monarch began a program of modernization for the beleaguered nation. Relations with Israel deteriorated in 2000, due to Jordan's widespread support for the Palestinian Intifada movement against Israel. Jordan remains one of the poorest of Arab nations.

GOVERNMENT
Website www.nic.gov.jo
Capital Amman
Type of government
Constitutional monarchy
Independence from Britain (UN Trust Territory)
May 25, 1946
Voting Universal adult suffrage
Head of state Monarch
Head of government Prime Minister
Constitution 1952
Legislature
Bicameral National Assembly
House of Deputies (lower house)
House of Notables (upper house)
Judiciary Court of Cassation
Member of
AL, IMF, UN, UNESCO, WHO, WTO

LAND AND PEOPLE
Land area 34,342 sq mi
(88,946 sq km)
Highest point Jabal Ram
5,755 ft (1,754 m)
Coastline 16 mi (26 km)
Population 5,307,470
Major cities and populations
Amman 990,000
Zarqa 405,000
Irbid 280,000
Ethnic groups
Arab 98%, Circassian 1%, others 1%
Religions Islam 95%,
Christianity 5%
Languages Arabic (official)

ECONOMIC
Currency Jordanian dinar
Industry
mining, petroleum refining, cement, potash, light manufacturing, tourism
Agriculture
wheat, barley, citrus, tomatoes, fruits, olives, sheep, goats, poultry
Natural resources
phosphates, potash, shale oil

Kazakhstan

KAZAKH REPUBLIC

Kazakhstan is located in central Asia, south of Russia between the Caspian Sea and China. Most of the country is low-lying plain. The northern landscape is part of the vast Siberian Plain. Mountains fringe the central plains on the east and southeast. The west is primarily the Caspian Depression, much of which lies below sea level. Most of the south is desert. Kazakhstan's climate varies enormously, from hot summers to very cold winters.

Kazakhs make up close to fifty percent of the population. Russians are the next largest ethnic group. The population is essentially an even split between Muslims and Christians. Kazakh is the national language, but Russian is the language of interethnic communication. Kazakhstan has a very high literacy rate.

Turkic tribes inhabited the region until overrun by the Mongols in the 1200s. Russia began encroaching on Kazakh territory by the sixteenth century. Russia began a program of forced migration of peasants from Russia to Kazakhstan in the nineteenth century.

The Kazakhs adopted a western-style government after the Russian Revolution of 1917. Three years later the Soviet Red Army blocked any further Kazakh independence. The country became the Kyrgyz Autonomous Soviet Socialist Republic in 1920. It was incorporated into the Soviet Union as the Kazakh Soviet Socialist Republic in 1936.

The Soviets launched a program of industrialization and large-scale agriculture. They also renewed the migration program, moving large numbers of Russians into the republic. The Baikonur Cosmodrome, in central Kazakhstan, was the base for the Soviet Union's space exploration program.

Kazakhstan saw major reforms with the collapse of the Soviet Union. The people voted for independence as a republic within the Commonwealth of Independent States (CIS) in 1991. Independence came on December 16, 1991, with Nursultan Nazarbayev as president.

Assisted by the European Union, industries were turned over to private ownership. The United States supported a program of removing old Soviet nuclear weapons which had been stored in Kazakhstan.

Nazarbayev continued in office through the 1990s despite widespread criticism of the electoral process. The capital moved from Almaty to Astana in 1997. Kazakhstan is presently developing new and better ways to utilize the country's energy resources. It is working to strengthen relationships with other countries.

GOVERNMENT
Website www.president.kz
Capital Astana
Type of government Republic
Independence from Soviet Union
December 16, 1991
Voting Universal adult suffrage
Head of state President
Head of government Prime Minister
Constitution 1995
Legislature
Bicameral Parliament
Majilis (lower house),
Senate (upper house)
Judiciary Supreme Court
Member of
CIS, IMF, UN, UNESCO, WHO

LAND AND PEOPLE
Land area 1,049,200 sq mi
(2,717,300 sq km)
Highest point
Khan Tangiri Shyngy
22,664 ft (6995 m)
Population 16,741,519
Major cities and populations
Almaty 1,200,000
Karaganda 600,000
Chimkent 405,000
Ethnic groups Kazakhs 46%,
Russians 35%, Germans 3%,
Uzbeks 2%, Tatars 2%
Religions Islam 48%,
Christianity 47%
Languages Kazakh (official),
Russian

ECONOMIC
Currency Tenge
Industry
mining, iron, steel, agricultural machinery, electric motors, construction materials
Agriculture
wheat, cotton, wool, livestock
Natural resources
petroleum, natural gas, coal, iron ore, manganese, chrome ore, nickel, cobalt, copper, molybdenum, lead, zinc, bauxite, gold, uranium

Kenya

REPUBLIC OF KENYA

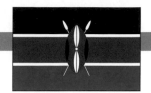

GOVERNMENT
Website www.kenya.go.ke
Capital Nairobi
Type of government Republic
Independence from Britain
December 12, 1963
Voting Universal adult suffrage
Head of state President
Head of government President
Constitution
1963, amended many times
Legislature
Unicameral National Assembly
(Bunge)
Judiciary High Court
Member of CN, IMF, OAU, UN,
UNESCO, WHO, WTO

LAND AND PEOPLE
Land area 224,960 sq mi
(582,946 sq km)
Highest point Mount Kenya
17,058 ft (5,199 m)
Coastline 334 mi (536 km)
Population 31,138,175
Major cities and populations
Nairobi 2.1 million
Mombasa 665,000
Nakura 219,000
Ethnic groups Kikuyu 22%,
Luhya 14%, Luo 13%, Kalenjin 12%,
Kamba 11%
Religions Christianity 70%,
traditional animism 20%, Islam 6%
Languages English, Swahili (both
official), indigenous languages

ECONOMIC
Currency Kenyan shilling
Industry
furniture, batteries, textiles, soap,
flour milling, agricultural
processing; oil refining, cement,
tourism, mining
Agriculture
coffee, tea, corn, wheat, sugar cane,
fruit, vegetables, dairy, beef, pork,
poultry
Natural resources
gold, limestone, soda ash, rubies,
fluorspar, garnets

Kenya is on the eastern coast of central Africa. The narrow, low-lying coastal strip rises from the Indian Ocean to a large, broad plateau. West of this area are great volcanic mountain chains, including the scrub-covered Kulal Mountains. In the west is the Great Rift Valley which runs north and south. The coastal climate is tropical. The inland areas are cooler with less rain.

Of Kenya's seventy ethnic groups, the largest are the Kikuyu, Luhya, Luo, Kalenjin, Kisii, Kamba and Meru. There are tiny minorities of Indians, Arabs and Europeans. Twenty percent of the people follow traditional animist religions. Muslims account for about six percent and the balance are Christian. English and Swahili are the official languages.

It is believed that immigrants from Ethiopia arrived in the area of Kenya around 2000 B.C. Trade was established with Arabs from the north by 100 B.C. They went on to establish many city-states for trading by the tenth century.

The Portugese controlled all trade in the area after its discovery by Vasco da Gama in 1498. A British and Dutch presence in the seventeenth century was thwarted as the city-states regained their independence.

A new wave of European explorers and missionaries arrived in the nineteenth century. The British East Africa Company came to dominate trade. Britain built a railway from Mombasa to Lake Victoria, opening up the interior for white-owned plantations. Kenya became a dependency of Britain in 1902.

Kenyan Mau Mau militants launched attacks on white settlers in the early 1950s. A state of emergency was declared. Kenyan African Union leader Jomo Kenyatta was imprisoned. His supporters were held in concentration camps.

Kenyatta began to negotiate independence after he was freed in 1961. Kenya's independence was declared on December 12, 1963. Kenyatta became the first president. His moderate government attracted foreign investors, which spurred economic progress.

Daniel Arap Moi, Kenyatta's successor, restricted foreign investment and increasingly suppressed opposition. Moi agreed to multi-party elections after riots in the early 1990s.

Terrorists linked to Osama bin Laden bombed the United States embassy in Nairobi in 1998, killing 250 people. Most attempts to reform the weak economy have failed. Moi's nominated successor, Uhuru Kenyatta, was defeated by Mwai Kibaki in the presidential elections of late December 2002.

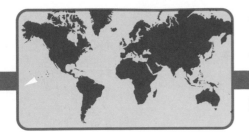

Kiribati

REPUBLIC OF KIRIBATI

Located in the central Pacific Ocean, Kiribati is made up of thirty-three coral islands and atolls. Kiribati has a tropical climate with a rainy season that lasts from October to May. The economy is primarily based on agriculture and fishing. Coconuts and palm products are the leading crops.

Most people of Kiribati are Micronesian, while a small number of them are Polynesian. Tarawa Island, the site of the naiton's capital, is very densely populated. Christianity is the dominant religion. English is the official language, although many people speak I-Kiribati, also known as Gilbertese.

The country has a unicameral legislature of 41 members, 39 of which are elected and 2 are appointed. The president is elected by the people for a four-year term.

The Micronesians of Kiribati can trace their heritage back to the first century A.D. Invasions by Fijians and Tongans altered the ethnic balance slightly during the fourteenth century. The culture remained otherwise unchanged for many years.

Spanish ships passed through the region in the sixteenth century. Europeans arrived in 1820, and the area became known as the Gilbert Islands. Plantations were established using forced local labor.

A slave trade developed. Gilbert islanders were sold as laborers to other Pacific islands and northern Australia. The discovery of phosphate on Ocean Island brought an even greater foreign interest to the area.

Slavery, along with deaths from new diseases brought to Kiribati, severely decreased the male population. Britain declared the Gilbert Islands and the nearby Ellice Islands a protectorate in 1916.

The island of Tarawa was the scene of an enormous battle during World War II. Allied forces, mostly United States Marines, launched gruelling attacks on entrenched Japanese forces. Canton Island became a regular refuelling point for airliners making the long flight from the United States to Australia during the 1950s.

Internal self-government was granted in the 1960s. The Ellice Islanders voted to separate from the other islands. The Gilbert Islands, the Phoenix Islands, Ocean Island, and eight of the Line Islands became the independent republic of Kiribati on July 12, 1979.

The problem of over-population is increasing, due to rising sea levels which are decreasing the size of the islands. The government has asked Australia and New Zealand to accept migrants from Kiribati to help ease this problem.

GOVERNMENT
Capital Bairiki, Tarawa
Type of government Republic
Independence from Britain
July 12, 1979
Voting Universal adult suffrage
Head of state President
Head of government President
Constitution 1979
Legislature
Unicameral Parliament
(Maneaba Ni Maungatabu)
Judiciary Court of Appeal
Member of CN, IMF, SPF, UN,
UNESCO, WHO

LAND AND PEOPLE
Land area 277 sq mi (717 sq km)
Highest point
unnamed location
266 ft (81 m)
Coastline
710 mi (1,143 km)
Population 96,335
Major cities and populations
Tarawa 29,000
Ethnic groups
I-Kiribati 97%
Religions Christianity 90%
Languages English (official),
I-Kiribati

ECONOMIC
Currency Australian dollar
Industry
fishing, handicrafts
Agriculture
copra, taro, breadfruit,
sweet potatoes, vegetables
Natural resources
seafood